Maurice Bardèche

Nuremberg
or the Promise Land

Ⓞmnia Veritas

MAURICE BARDÈCHE

Published in France:
"*Nuremberg ou la Terre Promise*", Paris 1948.

NUREMBERG OR THE PROMISE LAND

Published by
OMNIA VERITAS LTD

www.omnia-veritas.com

TRANSLATOR'S PREFACE 7

EPIGRAPH 13

   OTHER TITLES... 185

MAURICE BARDÈCHE

Translator's Preface

Maurice Bardèche's *Nuremberg or the Promised Land* was the first extended critique of the Nuremberg Trial. For a Frenchman to criticize that trial and especially the French role in it in 1948 took great courage: the book was banned in France, copies of it were seized, and Bardèche in 1952 was sentenced to a year in prison, although he spent only a few weeks there before being pardoned. His criticisms of the Nuremberg Trial have since been repeated by many others. In fact, just two years later in a subsequent work, *Nuremberg II ou les Faux Monnayeurs* (*Nuremberg II or the Counterfeiters*), Bardèche was able to cite a long list of others who had likewise criticized the fairness of that trial. Yet Bardèche's first book about Nuremberg remains something special, for it is much more than just a critique of the trial. It is the first work of Revisionism, and perhaps the only revisionist work that reads like great literature. It is a revisionist call-to-arms: it pleads for "history," but recognizes that it is still too early for the history of the war to be written: emotions are running too high. It cries out for objectivity, but does so while simmering with passion. It does not merely refute lies, it spits venom at the liars. It may with some justice be viewed as a polemic. Bardèche himself in effect admits it: "I needed to write it: that is my only excuse for this indiscretion."

But if it is a polemic, it is also very far from being a mere rant. Most of the book is in fact a painstakingly logical "criticism of testimony," specifically of the testimony produced by the French delegation at Nuremberg in support of the charge that during the occupation the Germans had tried to exterminate the French or, more exactly, had had a "will to exterminate." The charge is absurd and Bardèche easily demonstrates its absurdity. But its absurdity is what makes him so upset: he cannot forgive the French delegation that it will allow a future "German historian" to show that "France lied." Bardèche concentrates upon this part of the trial, however, not because the French were responsible for it and he is French but because it deals with events that he and his readers know firsthand and hence can judge whether the treatment of them at the trial was fair or not. He has heard reports about German atrocities in the East, about gas chambers, etc.; but about these things he reserves judgment. He wants evidence, and knows how easily reports are exaggerated and myths created.

Bardèche's book is a revisionist classic. It is not however, in my opinion, of interest today primarily because of its contribution to Revisionism nor because of anything it says about the past, but rather because of what it says about the future. Throughout the first three quarters of the book the discussion of the trial is interlaced with somber warnings and ominous admonitions to the reader: "One is proposing a future to us, one does so by condemning the past. It is into this future also that we want to see clearly. It is these principles that we would like to look at directly. For we already foresee that these new ethics refer to a strange universe, a universe with something sick about it, an elastic universe where our eyes no longer recognize things." The presence of these warnings and admonitions to the reader gives the book an oracular tone. Bardèche has examined the transcript of the Nuremberg Trial and now, like an ancient prophet after examining the entrails of a sacrifice, he has bad news to deliver and knows that others will not want to hear him. Indeed, very few have been willing to hear him. The last quarter of the book is devoted entirely to an exposition of what the future will bring. That anyone in 1948 could have foreseen so accurately our modern world is to me astounding. Bardèche recognized that the judicial travesty at Nuremberg was not simply an act of vengeance by victors against the vanquished and that what was on trial there was not just the particular German defendants, nor the German nation, nor even National Socialism, but rather nationalism itself: the idea that a people own the land that they have long lived in and have the right to live in it as they wish and to exclude others from living in it if they so wish. It is nationalism in any form which was condemned at Nuremberg.

With amazing prescience Bardèche foresaw in its condemnation the coming of an international system which is first and foremost economic, not political or governmental. Its purpose is to protect an international economic élite, not ordinary persons, or peoples or nations. It offers the latter lots of rights but no guarantees that these rights will be respected. Its laws are unclear (unlike those of a prince) and broadly unenforceable, but the system does not attempt to enforce them broadly but only selectively. For selected victims punishments are severe. Victims are selected not so much because they have broken laws but because they have offended the "universal conscience," the conscience created and fostered in us all by the media (Bardèche's "radio"). Bardèche clearly foresaw the system which we today call "globalism," although he nowhere uses that term.

He also foresaw at least implicitly many other aspects of our world: third world immigration, the irrational glorification of democracy, loss of sovereignty, humanitarian wars and interference, hate crimes, affirmative action, racial miscegenation and replacement, etc.: "At the bottom of the sanctuary there sits a Negro god. You have all the rights, except to speak evil of the god." "And, from one end of the world to the other, in perfectly similar cities... there will live under similar laws a bastard population, a race of indefinable and gloomy slaves, without genius, without instinct, without voice... But this will be the promised land."

In 1949, one year after the publication of *Nuremberg or the Promised Land*, another prophetic book was published, George Orwell's novel *Nineteen Eighty-Four*. In it Orwell describes a scary future in which there is a single party dictatorship, living conditions are drab, food is scarce, people's thoughts are openly controlled by Big Brother, their words and actions are monitored through "telescreens" which they cannot turn off, they are given no choice over what they view on these screens, there is only one channel on the "telescreens" and one film (always a war film) in the theatres, in one such film refugees trying to escape are shot to the delight of the audience, some of these refugees are Jewish, "the Enemy of the People" is a Jew, Emmanuel Goldstein, who is condemned for "advocating freedom of speech, freedom of the Press, freedom of assembly, freedom of thought," people are openly taught to hate him and his followers during "Two Minutes Hate" and "Hate Week," sex is discouraged through a "Junior Anti- Sex League," the Inner Party is called the "Inner Party," thoughtcrime is called "thoughtcrime," Thought Police are called "Thought Police," the media propagate obvious, self-contradictory lies such as: "War Is Peace," "Freedom Is Slavery," "Ignorance Is Strength," people are told that democracy is "impossible" (although the Party is said to be its "guardian"), capitalism is viewed as a barbarity that has "vanished."

The world described in *1984* little resembles that in the Occident today. We live in multi-party democracies. Our mainstream media tell us not only that democracy is possible and a very good thing, but that its triumph everywhere is virtually inevitable, an inevitability which we should make every effort to encourage. Living conditions are generally good, food is abundant. Capitalism is alive and well and is promoted as an economic panacea. Our politicians advocate the same things as does Emmanuel Goldstein. Our media propagate obvious lies such as: "Diversity is our strength," but they at least avoid flagrant self-contradictions (some kinds of diversity may indeed be a source of strength, although certainly not the radical ethnic diversity that our media promote). Refugees do not flee our societies, but rather risk their lives trying to get into them. We are not taught to hate, but to tolerate. Sex is not generally discouraged, even among the young. With our multi-channel televisions and the internet we are free to see, hear, read, and discuss almost anything, if not everywhere. Freedom reigns. Yet to some that freedom seems, if not illusory, useless. It is useless because people's thoughts and actions are monitored and controlled not by anything outside themselves but by their own warped consciences, consciences deliberately warped by our mainstream media, consciences closely resembling Bardèche's "universal conscience."

Orwell's and Bardèche's books have had quite different careers in the Occident. Orwell's, although formerly banned in the Soviet Union, has been widely read and praised; Bardèche's is still banned in France and is generally unknown elsewhere. *1984* has served to warn us against the dangers of Communism, and for that deserves acclaim. But one cannot help but wonder if its general acclaim today is not also an index to its irrelevance. We have escaped the dreadful future envisioned by Orwell in *1984*. We have not escaped the dreadful future envisioned by Bardèche in 1948. Bardèche says that his "only ambition, in writing this book, was to be able to read it again without shame in fifteen years." My ambition, in translating it, was much more grandiose: I hope to hear it read some day without shame on TV by a politician. Bardèche wrote this book for the sake of the German "reprobates," whom "the radios of all the people of the world, and the presses of all the people of the world, and millions of voices from all the horizons of the world" characterize as "monsters." I have translated it also for the sake of "reprobates," those nationalists throughout the Occident whom all our radios and presses and millions of voices likewise characterize as little better than "monsters."

G. F. H.

Epigraph

Solomon counted all the foreigners who were in the country of Israel and whose enumeration had been made by David, his father. One found one hundred fifty-three thousand six hundred of them. And it took seventy thousand of them to carry the burdens, eighty thousand to cut the stones in the mountain, and three thousand six hundred to supervise and make the people work.

Second Book of Chronicles, 2, 17-18.

I am not taking up the defense of Germany. I am taking up the defense of the truth. I do not know if the truth exists, and many people have made arguments to prove to me that it does not. But I know that lies exist; I know that the systematic deformation of facts exists. We have lived for three years with a falsification of history. This falsification is skilful: it involves fantasies, it is even based on a conspiracy of imagined fantasies.

One started by saying: here is all that you have suffered, then one says: remember what you have suffered. They have even invented[1] a philosophy for this falsification. It consists of explaining to us that what we really were does

---

[1] Numbers enclosed in brackets like this occur in the French text available on line at the AAARGH website; they refer to page numbers in the original text. I have retained them here to facilitate reference to these two texts.

not have any importance; that what matters is only **the image** which is made of us. It appears that this transposition is **the only reality**. The Rothschild group is thus promoted to a metaphysical existence.

Me, I believe stupidly in the truth. I even believe that it ends up triumphing over all and even over the image which one makes of us. The precarious destiny of the falsification invented by the Resistance has already brought us proof of this. Today the block is broken, its colors are peeling off: these billboards last only a few seasons. But then if the democracies' propaganda has lied about us for three years, if it has distorted what we did, why should we believe it when it talks to us about Germany? Did it not falsify the history of the occupation just as it mispresented the actions of the French government? Public opinion is beginning to correct its judgment about the purification.[2]

Should we not ask ourselves whether the same revision is not to be made about the condemnations brought by these same judges at Nuremberg? Is it not at least honest, indeed necessary, to raise this question? If the judicial action which struck thousands of French is a fraud, what proves to us that that which condemned thousands of Germans is not also a fraud? Do we have the right not even to be interested in this issue?

Will we allow thousands of men, at this very time, to suffer and to be outraged at our refusal to testify, at our

---

[2] *Purification* the punishment of collaborators in France after the occupation.

cowardice, at our false commiseration? They push away this straight jacket in which we wish to put their voice and their past; they know that our newspapers lie, that our films lie, that our writers lie, they know it and will not forget it: will we endure these looks of disdain which they rightly shoot at us? The whole history of this war is to be redone, we know it. Will we refuse to open our door to the truth?

We have seen these men staying in our houses and our cities; they were our enemies and, what is more painful, they were the masters on our premises. That does not take away from them the right which all men have to truth and justice, their right to the honesty of other men. They fought with courage; they have undergone the fortune of war and have accepted it; today, their cities are destroyed, they live in holes in the middle of ruins, they have nothing any more, they live as beggars on what little the victor concedes to them, their children die and their daughters are spoils for foreigners, their distress exceeds all that men could ever have imagined. Will we refuse them bread and salt? And if these beggars whom we treat as banished men were men not different from ourselves? If our hands were not purer than their hands, if our consciences were not lighter than their consciences? If we had been mistaken? If we had been lied to? It is however on the basis of this sentence without appeal that the victors ask us to found a dialogue with Germany, or rather to refuse to have one. They have seized the sword of Jehovah, and they have driven the Germans from the realm of humanity. The collapse of Germany was not enough for the victors. The Germans were not just a defeated people, for they were not an ordinary defeated people. It is Evil which had been overcome in them: one had to teach them that they were Barbarians, that they were **the Barbarians**.

What happened to them, the last degree of distress, desolation as on the day of the flood, their country swallowed up like Gomorrah, with them wandering about alone, amazed, in the middle of ruins, as though shortly after the collapse of the world, one had to teach them that **this was well done**, as children say. It was a just punishment sent from heaven. They had to sit down, these Germans, on their ruins and beat their chests. For they had been monsters. And it is just that the cities of the monsters are destroyed, and also the women of the monsters and their little children. And the radios of all the people of the world, and the presses of all the people of the world, and millions of voices from all the horizons of the world, without exception, without a false note, have begun to explain to the man seated on his ruins why he had been a monster.

This book is addressed to these reprobates. For it is necessary that they know that not everyone has blindly accepted the victors' verdict. The time to make an appeal will come some day. Courts that follow a victory by arms can pass only transitory sentences. Political opportunism and fear already begin to revoke these judgments. Our opinion about Germany and the National-Socialist regime is independent of these contingencies. Our only ambition, in writing this book, was to be able to read it again without shame in fifteen years. When we find that the German army or the National-Socialist Party committed crimes, naturally we will call them crimes. But when we think that one makes these accusations by means of sophisms or lies, we will denounce these sophisms and these lies. For all this looks a bit too much like theatre-lighting: one directs projectors and one lights up only the stage, meanwhile all the rest of the place is in the dark. It is time that the chandeliers be lit and that we take a close look at the spectators.

*****

Let us note initially, as a starting point, that this legal action against Germany, or more exactly against National-Socialism, has a solid basis, a basis much more solid than one generally believes. Only, it is not that proclaimed. And things, in truth, are much more dramatic than they are said to be: the basis for the charge, the motive behind the charge, is actually much more distressing for the victors.

Public opinion and the prosecutors for the victorious powers affirm that they have set themselves up as judges because they represent civilization. That is the official explanation. But that is also the official sophism, for that is to take as a first principle and a certainty what is precisely under discussion. It is at the end of an open trial between Germany and the Allies that one would be able to say which camp represented civilization. It is not at the beginning that one can say that, and above all it is not one of the parties on trial who can say it. The United States, England and the U.S.S.R. brought in their most erudite lawyers to support this childish argument. For four years our radios have repeated: "you are barbarians, you were overcome, and therefore you are barbarians." For it is clear that Mr. Shawcross, Mr. Jackson and Mr. Rudenko speak no differently at their desks at Nuremberg when they proclaim the unanimous indignation of the civilized world, the indignation that their own propaganda caused, supported, guided, and which can be directed by them at will, like a swarm of locusts, against any form of political life which may displease them. However, let us make no mistake about it, this prefabricated indignation has long been and, all in all, still is the principal basis for the charge against the German regime. It is the indignation of the civilized world which requires the trial, it is that too which supports its conduct, it is in the end everything: the judges at Nuremberg are only the secretaries, the scribes of this unanimity. One puts on us by force some red glasses and then invites us to declare that things are red. Now there is a program with a future for which we have not finished counting the philosophical merits!

But the truth is very different. The true basis for the Nuremberg Trial, the one which no one has ever dared to point out, is, I suspect, not fear: it is the spectacle of the ruins, it is the panic of the victors. **It is necessary that the others be in the wrong.** It is necessary, for if, by chance, they had not been monsters, how would the victors bear the weight of all those destroyed cities, and those thousands of phosphorus bombs? It is the horror, it is the despair of the victors which is the true motive for the trial. They have veiled their faces before what they were forced to do and, to give themselves courage, they transformed their massacres into a crusade. They invented *a posteriori* a right to massacre in the name of respect for humanity. Being killers, they promoted themselves to policemen. After a certain number of deaths, we know that any war becomes obligatorily a war of the Right (*Droit*).[3] The victory is thus complete only if,

---

[3] The word "droit" occurs 154 times in this text; it usually means "law" or "right" (in the sense of "a legal or moral right to do something"). *Le droit* also sometimes, as here, seems to mean "the right" in the sense of "what is right," i.e., what is both legally and morally right (a sense not exactly recognized in the dictionaries). It is not

after having taken over the citadel by force, one also takes over the consciences by force. From this point of view, the Nuremberg Trial is an apparatus of modern war which deserves to be described like a bomber.

We had already tried to do the same thing in 1918, but then, the war having been only a costly military operation, one had been satisfied with palming off on the Germans the aggression card. Nobody wanted to be responsible for so many deaths. We made the vanquished do this by obliging their negotiators to sign a statement that their country had been responsible for the war. This time around, the war having become on both sides a massacre of innocents, it was not enough to obtain that the vanquished recognize themselves as the aggressors. To excuse the crimes committed in conducting the war, it was absolutely necessary to discover some even more serious ones on the other side. It was absolutely necessary that the English and American bombers seem the sword of the Lord. The Allies did not have a choice. If they did not solemnly affirm, if they did not prove by any means whatever that they had been the saviors of humanity, they were nothing more than murderers. If, one day, men ceased believing in the **German**

---

always easy to determine which of these three senses of *droit* is appropriate. For that reason I have sometimes indicated in the translation, as here, where *droit* occurs: the reader can then decide for himself which is the appropriate meaning. (*Il diritto* in Italian and *das Recht* in German carry the same meanings as *le droit* and have greatly factilitated the work of Bardèche's Italian and German translators.) The word *loi*, which also means "law," occurs 49 times in the text. For the sake of clarity, I have sometimes also indicated in the translation where it occurs.

monstrosity, would they not demand an accounting for the devastated cities?

There is thus an obvious interest on the part of British and American propaganda and, to a lesser degree, of Soviet propaganda, to support the thesis of **German crimes**. This will become even more obvious if one keeps in mind that, in spite of its publicity value, this thesis obtained its definitive form only rather late.

In the beginning, nobody believed it. Radio broadcasts endeavored to justify entry into the war. Public opinion indeed feared a German hegemony, but it did not believe in a **German monstrosity**. During the first months of the occupation the officers said: "They are not going to hit us again with that stuff about German atrocities." The bombardments of Coventry and London, the first air raids on civilian populations, spoiled this bit of wisdom. And so too, a little later, the submarine war. Then the occupation, hostages, and reprisals. And then with the help of radio broadcasts public opinion managed to reach the first degree of intoxication. The Germans were monsters because they were unfair adversaries and because they believed only in the law of the strongest. Opposite them: the correct nations which were always beaten because they conducted themselves in everything with honesty. But people did not really believe that the Germans were monsters; they saw in all this only the same themes of propaganda which had circulated at the time of the Kaiser and Big Bertha.[4]

---

[4] *Big Bertha* the biggest German artillery gun in World War I, with a calibre of 420 mm. (16.5 in.).

The occupation of the territories in the East and, at the same time, the fight undertaken in all Europe against terrorism and sabotage provided other arguments. The Germans were monsters because they were everywhere followed by their killers; the myth of the Gestapo was put on its pedestal: in all Europe, the German armies installed the reign of terror, the nights were haunted by the sounds of boots, the prisons were full, and at each dawn shots rang out. The purpose of this war became clear: millions of men, from one end of the continent to the other, fought for the liberation of the new slaves; bombers were given the name "Liberator." This was the time when America entered the war. People did not yet believe that the Germans were monsters, but they did already view the war as a crusade for *freedom*. That was the second stage of intoxication.

But these images did not yet correspond to the voltage of our current propaganda. The retreat of the German armies in the East finally made it possible to give the word. It was the moment that they were waiting for: for the German reflux left wrecks. There was talk of war crimes, and a declaration on October 30, 1943 permitted the public, to everyone's general satisfaction, to learn of these crimes and to foresee their punishment. This time, the Germans were certainly monsters, they cut off the hands of little children, just as had always been said. It was no longer just force, it was cruelty. From this moment, the civilized world had **rights** (*droits*) **against them**: for in the end there are some delicate consciences who do not admit that one should punish treachery by air raids or that one should regard an authoritative regime as a crime against common law (*droit*), whereas everyone is ready to punish executioners of children and to place them outside the laws (*droits*) of war. They were caught in the act red-handed. This idea was diffused and exploited. People started to think that the Germans could very well be monsters, and so they reached the third stage of intoxication, which consists of forgetting what was being done each night in the air-raids by thinking angrily about what was happening each day in the prisons.

This was the military situation which they had desired since the start, in order to be able to manipulate people's minds. And for this same reason this situation needed to be maintained. It became all the more necessary when, shortly after this date, in December 1943, the methods of bombardment changed: instead of having military targets, the Allied aviators received the order to adopt the tactic of carpet bombing which destroyed whole cities. These apocalyptic destructions required, obviously, a corresponding monstrosity. One felt so strongly the need for this that they set up, as of this date, a powerful organization for the detection of German crimes, whose mission it was to move in on the heels of the first waves of the occupation, just as the formations of police followed the advance of the armored troops into Russia. This analogy is suggestive: the Germans ethnically cleansed, the Americans accused, each went about their business with great urgency. The Allies' investigations, as one knows, were crowned with success. They had the good fortune in January 1945 to discover the concentration camps of which no one had heard until then, and which became precisely the proof that one needed, an obvious offence in a pure form, **the crime against humanity** which justified all. They were photographed, they were filmed, they appeared in many publications, they were made known by a gigantic publicity campaign, like a brand of pen. The moral war was won. The **German monstrosity** was proven to be a fact by these invaluable documents. The people who had invented the camps did not have the right to complain about anything. And the silence was such, the curtain had been so abruptly, so skilfully pulled away, that not a voice dared to say that all this was too good to be perfectly true.

It was thus that German culpability was affirmed at different times by different reasons; and it should be noted that this culpability increased as the bombardments of civilians multiplied. This synchronism is in itself rather suspect, and it is all too clear that we should not approve without scrutiny the charges of governments which have so obvious a need for a currency of exchange.

It is perhaps useful to point out that in technical terms the trial was an admirable production. After having presented our most sincere compliments to the technicians, Jewish for the most part, who orchestrated this program, we would like to be able to see clearly and to find our way around in this *pièce à tiroirs*,[5] where the accusations arrive just in the nick of time like dramatic reversals in a melodrama. Thus it is to this task that we will stick. And, of course, this small book can only be a first stone. It will contain more questions than assertions, more analyses than documents. But is that not at least something: to put a little order in a matter which they have willfully presented in a confused manner? They have done their work so well that today no one dares any more to call things by their proper

---

[5] *pièce à tiroirs* an "episodic play," usually with a light theme.

names. Everything altogether is called monstrous: the acts, the men, the ideas. People's minds now are stupified, they are benumbed, inert, they grope about in a wadding of lies. And sometimes, when they meet truths, they back away with horror, for these truths are proscribed. The first object of our concern will thus be a kind of restoration of the evidence. But this work of correction should not be limited to the mere facts of the case. The Nuremberg Court judged in the name of a certain number of principles, in the name of a certain political ethics. There is a reverse side to all these accusations. One is proposing a future to us, one does so by condemning the past. It is into this future also that we want to see clearly. It is these principles that we would like to look at directly. For we already foresee that these new ethics refer to a strange universe, a universe with something sick about it, an elastic universe where our eyes no longer recognize things: but a universe which is that of others, precisely that of which Bernanos[6] had a presentiment when he feared that one day the dreams, locked up in the sly brain of a small Negro shoeshiner in a New York ghetto, would come true. We are there. Our minds are doped. We have been struck by Circe. We have all become Jewish.

* * * * *

Let us start then by describing this Nuremberg Trial, at the top of which rises the Acropolis of this new city.[7] It is

---

[6] *Bernanos* Georges Bernanos, French right-wing Catholic writer, best known for his novel, *Diary of a Country Priest* (1936).

[7] The word in the French text which I have translated here as "city" is *cité*. It occurs thirty-one times in the text. For the sake of consistency, I translate it elsewhere also

there that the charges end up, and it is there that begins the future world.

The secretariat of the International Military Tribunal began last year to publish the shorthand transcript of the Nuremberg Trial. This publication is supposed to run to twenty-four quarto volumes of approximately 500 to 700 pages. The French edition currently includes twelve volumes, which deal primarily with the documents accompanying the accusation. This part of the work will be enough for us. For the accusation judges itself by what it itself says. It seems to me unnecessary even to hear the defense.

Let us point out initially some structural elements. The International Military Tribunal was established by the London Agreement of August 8, 1945 between France, the United States, Great Britain and the Union of the Soviet Socialist Republics. To this agreement was appended a *Statute of the Tribunal* which determined at the same time the composition, the operation, the rules of the court and **the list of actions which were to be regarded as criminal.** One thus learned for the first time, from this statute published on August 8, 1945, that certain acts which had

---

as "city," although in some cases it might perhaps be better translated as "community," "city-state," or "state." In any case, the reader should be aware that *cité* does not mean "city" in the sense of "urban area." The word conveys no contrast between urban and rural; it rather denotes the civil body of which one is a citizen (*citoyen*). There is another word *ville* which I have also translated as "city"; it occurs thirty-nine times. It means what "city" does in English and, like "city," may or may not denote a distinction between urban and rural.

not been mentioned up to then in the texts of international law were to be regarded as criminal, and that the defendants would have to answer for acts such as these, although it had never been written anywhere before that they were criminal. It was learned there, moreover, that the immunity which covered executants of received orders would not be taken into account, and that, in addition, the court could declare that any political organization arraigned before it was not a political organization, but rather a criminal conspiracy assembled to perpetrate a plot or a crime, and that consequently all its members could be treated as conspirators or criminals.

The trial went on for a year, from October 1945 to October 1946. The Court consisted of three judges, the first American, the second French, and the third Russian, and it was chaired by a high-ranking British magistrate, Lord Justice Lawrence. The charges were prosecuted by four Attorney Generals assisted by forty-nine magistrates in uniform. An important secretariat had been put in charge of the gathering and classification of documents. There were four counts in the indictment: **conspiracy** (that is, the political actions of the National-Socialist party from the time of its origin, since its actions were comparable to a conspiracy), **crime against peace** (that is, the charge of having caused the war), **crimes of war** and **crimes against humanity**. The indictment was supported by means of a series of reports by the Public Ministry; each of these reports included the introduction of documents which were published following the trial. Everyone knows, since the press has explained it at length, that these reports were made in front of a microphone; they had to be pronounced slowly, each sentence being separated from the following one by a pause. Translators translated at once. The defendants, their lawyers and the members of the Public Ministry had earphones which enabled them to hear the debates in their language, just by tuning in the frequency of the broadcast of their particular translator. This technical virtuosity is what struck people's fancies the most. And yet, when one thinks of it, that is not what was most surprising at the trial.

The appearances of justice were maintained perfectly. The defense had few rights, but these rights were respected. Some overzealous auxiliaries of the Public Ministry were called to order for having allowed themselves prematurely to characterize the acts about which they were reporting. The court stopped the report of the French Public Ministry because of its unfair and diffuse character, and refused to hear the rest of it. Several defendants were discharged. In the end the forms were perfectly well observed, and never was a more debatable justice rendered with more propriety.

For this modern machinery, as one knows, had the result of resurrecting a jurisprudence like that of Negro tribes. The victorious king is set on his throne and has his witchdoctors called in: then, in the presence of warriors sitting on their heels, someone cuts the throats of the vanquished chiefs. We start to suspect that all the rest is a bit of comedy, and the public, after eighteen months, is no longer taken in by this kind of play-acting. The chiefs have their throats cut because they were vanquished; the atrocities with which one reproaches them, well, no just man can avoid saying to himself that the commanders of the Allied armies could be reproached with atrocities just as serious: the phosphorus bombs well counterbalance the concentration camps. An American court which condemns Göring to death has no more authority, in the eyes of men, than would a German court which presumed to condemn Roosevelt. A court which creates the law after being seated on its bench brings us back to the beginning of history. One did not dare to judge so at the time of Chilperic.[8] The law of the strongest is a more honest way. When the Gaul shouts *Vae victis*,[9] at least he does not take himself for Solomon. But this court succeeded in being an assembly of Negroes in starched collars: this is the plan for our future civilization. It is a masquerade, a nightmare: they are dressed as judges, they are serious, they are capped with ear-phones, they have the heads of patriarchs, they read papers with a saccharine voice in four languages at the same time, but in reality they are Negro kings, it is a costume party for Negro kings, and in the icy and staid room one can almost hear in the background the war drums of the tribes. They are very clean Negroes and perfectly modernized. And they have obtained without knowing it, in their Negro naiveté and in their Negro unconsciousness, a result that none of them undoubtedly had envisaged: they have rehabilitated by their bad faith even those whose defense was almost impossible, and they have given to millions of destitute German refugees , ennobled by defeat and their condition as the vanquished, the right to scorn them. Göring mocked them, for he well knew that they were rendering him right in everything, since they, with their panoply of judges, were paying homage to

---

[8] *Chilperic* a sixth century King of the Franks, specifically, the King of Neustria from 561 to his death in 581.

[9] *Vae Victis* "Woe to the Conquered," the words of Brennus, the King of the Gauls, who conquered Rome in 390 B.C. Cf. Livy, *Ab Urbe Condita* 5.34-49.

the law of the strongest, on which he had based his own law. Göring laughed to see Göring disguised as a judge judge Göring disguised as a convict.

But the crude and external aspects of this legal comedy are not what really interests us. That the judgment of German chiefs by American chiefs was a political error is something about which most people agree today, including part of the American press. But that was only one political error among many. That the Nuremberg Court was basically a summary form of justice is of little importance. On the contrary, that which seems to us much more important and that for which we much more reproach the Nuremberg judges is that they were not satisfied to be executors of summary justice: it is their claim to be truly judges that we dispute; their defenders defend them on this basis, and it is on this basis that we attack them. We thus will examine their claim to be judges. We call to the Court of the Truth not those American statesmen who foolishly condemned the German statesman who signed with them the agreement of capitulation; we call rather the Universal Conscience to serve as our judge. Since they say that they are wisdom, we will pretend, indeed, to take them for wise men; since they say that they are the law, we will accept them for a moment as legislators: let us then penetrate into the gardens of the new law by following there Mr. Shawcross, Justice Jackson and Mr. Rudenko: these are lands that are full of wonders.

*****

Let us start by noting that we cannot simply ignore these lands. The voyage of discovery that we will make is something that should stir our emotions since this universe cannot be neglected. It is that in which we are going to live. It is the Germans who are the defendants, but it is everyone, in the end it is we ourselves who are liable (*les assujettis*): for all that we will do contrary to the legal precedents set at Nuremberg is from now on a crime and could be charged against us. This trial has proclaimed the Law of Nations, of which no one is supposed to be unaware. Eight hundred thousand Chinese will perhaps be hung in ten years in the name of this Nuremberg statute, since two hundred thousand Germans are now held in concentration camps in honor of the Briand- Kellog Pact about which they perhaps have never heard.

The first terrace onto which the new gardens of the Law extend is a completely modern conception of responsibility. We believed up to now that we would have to answer only for our own acts, and it is on the basis of this principle that we founded our humble religions. This principle is today out-of-date. To give a stable basis for the morals of international law, they have based them on collective responsibility.

Pay special attention to me here. The Nuremberg judges never said that the German people were collectively responsible for the acts of the National-Socialist regime; they have even asserted several times the opposite. The German people are condemned as a whole in the **opinion** of civilized peoples, they are objects of **horror,** but the judges themselves affect serenity and officially do not accuse them as a whole. However, the **Law** of peoples is like a tax: for there to be a tax, there first has to be a taxable product. So for there to be a judgment, it is necessary first that there be culprits, and it is intolerable that in the end one find only a hierarchy, which leads to only one chief who is responsible and who plays on you the nasty trick of committing suicide. That is why the new Law **initially** describes the general citizenry thus: "the guilty include all those who belong to a 'criminal organization.'"

Nothing could be more reasonable. It is, however, here that the difficulties start, for these notions of the new Law are all somewhat vague, they are infinitely extensible. A criminal organization is somewhat like a detective novel: it is only at the end that you know the culprit. Thus, the executives of the National-Socialist Party constitute a criminal organization, but the executives of the Communist Party, who much resemble them, do not constitute a criminal organization. The men in both cases, however, have the same temperament. They employ the same methods, and in both cases with the same fanaticism: they also strive toward the same end which is the dictatorship of the party. There is thus nothing in their composition or, as the philosophers say, in their essence, which distinguishes these two groups from each other. There is nothing in their conduct either which does this, for historians claim that those in charge of the Communist Party have no more control over human life and human freedom than do those in charge of the National-Socialist Party. Will we have to humbly conclude that we condemn the ones because we have them under our boot and that we do not put the others on trial because they would laugh at us? That however is a hypothesis which cannot be eliminated. The jurisdiction of international law is limited to weak or defeated countries. It calls a disadvantage (*inconvénient*) among strong peoples what it calls a crime among the defeated. This is radically different from penal or civil jurisdiction, in the sense that it cannot reach certain acts and consequently is impotent to establish a truly universal characterization of these acts. This justice is like daylight: it clarifies only half of the inhabited lands.

Its impotence is its least defect, for there is good faith in the impotence.[10] But international law is a slave, moreover, to political contingencies: there are judgments which it does not want to pronounce. The political leaders of the Communist Party could as a group be condemned on paper by a court unable to have its sentence carried out: that would be less serious than to see a court deliberately ignore the obvious similarity of the Communist leaders as a group to the National-Socialist leaders as a group. It is all too clear that there is not and cannot be a justice for all. It is no longer justice: "according to whether you are powerful or destitute," but: "according to whether you are in one camp or the other." One realizes then that criminal character is transposed from essence to finality, and not even to the true final purpose of the organization, to its distant final purpose (since the court is very far from officially admitting the progressist character of the Stalinist dictatorship), but rather to a near final purpose of which the court is the only judge.[11]

---

[10] That is, its good faith (i.e. its desire to punish all the guilty) is compatible with its failure to punish some since it is simply incapable of punishing some.

[11] Bardèche employs here the Aristotelian distinction between formal and final causes. The formal cause of something is its essence or form; the final cause is its purpose. Bardèche complicates the discussion by adding his own distinction between near and distant final causes/purposes. What the passage means is basically this: in international law what constitutes a crime is not what an organization actually is or does (= essence, form, formal cause) but what its purpose is (= final cause/purpose). And, for the Nuremberg Court, what the purpose of an organization is is not its real

The same acts are not criminal any more by definition and in themselves, they are or are not criminal according to a certain optics: the deportations which in the end serve the cause of democracy are not perceived by the new jurisdiction to be criminal acts, while any deportation by the enemies of the democracy is indeed criminal. Thus the court takes, as it were, a refracted view of these acts, like how one sees sticks in water: from one angle they are straight, from another crooked.

That makes life quite difficult for us others, for us private individuals. For the result is that no one is ever sure of not belonging to a criminal organization. A German shoemaker, father of three children, ex-combatant at Verdun, who took out in 1934 a Nazi Party membership card, was accused by the Public Ministry of belonging to a criminal organization. But what of a French tradesman, father of three children, ex-combatant at Verdun, who joined the movement Croix de Feu?[12] How is what he did any different from what the German did? Both believed they were supporting a political movement intended to assure the rebuilding of their country. Both performed the same act: and yet the course of events has given to each of these acts a different value. One is a patriot (provided that he listened to

---

purpose (= distant final purpose, e.g., dictatorship), but rather its ostensible purpose (= near final purpose, e.g., liberation of the proletariat). The court refuses to recognize that although the Stalinist regime may have initially pursued the (near final) purpose of liberating the proletariat, in the course of time it began to pursue almost exclusively the (distant final) purpose of dictatorship.

[12] *Croix de Feu* Cross of Fire: a far right anti-Communist group of French veterans.

English radio broadcasts, of course), but the other is accused by the representatives of the universal conscience.

These difficulties are of an extreme gravity. The ground is stolen from under our feet. Perhaps our expert jurists are unaware of it, but they are adopting a completely modern conception of justice, that which served as a basis for the Moscow trials in the U.S.S.R. Our conception of justice had been until now Roman and Christian: Roman, in that it requires that any punishable act have an invariable description which goes to the very essence of the act, whereby is made clear what is done and by whom; Christian, in that the intention was always to be taken into account, either to aggravate or attenuate the circumstances surrounding the act qualified as a crime. But there is another conception of culpability which can be called Marxist for several reasons: it consists in thinking that such and such an act which was not wrong in itself nor in its intention, at the moment when it was done, can legitimately seem wrong from a certain posterior point of view of the events. This is what they literally say. The Marxists are in good faith in saying this, for they live in a kind of non-Euclidean world where the lines of history appear grouped and deformed or, if you prefer, harmonized by the Marxist prospective. Mr. Shawcross and Justice Jackson, the English and American prosecutors, however, live in an Euclidean world where all is sure, where all is clear, or where at least all should be sure and clear, and where the facts should be the facts and nothing more. It is their bad faith alone which transports us into a world where nothing is sure. Our intentions do not count any more, even our acts do not count any more, what we are does not really count any more, but our own history, and our own life, can from now on be kneaded, stretched, and puffed up by a kind of political demiurge,[13] a potter who will lend them forms which they never had. Each one of our actions in the world that is being prepared for us is as a soap bubble which history holds at the end of its blowtorch: history can give it the form and the coloring which it wants, and a judge may then come forward and say to us: "You are no longer a German shoe-maker or a French tradesman as you believed to be; you are a monster, you belonged to a criminal conspiracy, you took part in a plot against peace, as the first section of my bill of indictment indicates very clearly."

What will we answer to the Germans if they say to us one day that they do not see anything monstrous in National-Socialism itself, that this regime may have committed some excesses, as happens in all wars and each time that a regime must entrust to elements of a police force the task of protecting it from sabotage, but that none of all this has anything to do with the essence of National-Socialism and that they continue to think that they fought for justice and truth, for what they regarded then and continue to regard now as justice and truth? What will we answer to these men against whom we have made a religious war? They too have their saints, what will we answer to their saints? When one of them recalls to us this immense harvest of grandeur and sacrifice that young Germany offered with all its force, when these thousands of ears of corn, so beautiful, are presented to us, before the new harvest, what

---

[13] *Demiurge* "craftsman": the creator in Plato's *Timaeus*, who creates by giving forms to previously unformed matter.

will we say, we accessories of the judges, accessories to lies? We judged in the name of a certain notion of human progress. Who guarantees us that this notion is right? It is only one religion like any other. Who guarantees us that this religion is true? Half of humanity says to us already that it is false, that they are ready, they also, to die like witnesses for another faith. What was true then? Is it our religion or that of the Soviet Socialist Republics? And if no one can know yet who among the judges grasped the truth, what is the value of this absolute in whose name we have spread destruction and misfortune? What proves to us that National- Socialism was not also the truth? What proves to us that we did not take for its essence what were just contingencies, inevitable accidents of combat, as we do perhaps also for communism, or is it that we have simply lied? And what if National-Socialism had actually been truth and progress, or at least, a form of truth and of progress? What if the future world could be built only by a choice between communism and authoritative nationalism, if the concept of democracy were not viable, if it were condemned by history? We admit that what is essential is to save civilization and that, to make it triumph, it may be necessary to crush cities; what if National-Socialism were also one of those chariots which carry the gods and whose wheels may need to pass over thousands of bodies, if that is necessary? The bombs prove nothing against an idea. If we one day crush Soviet Russia, will communism be any less true? Who can be sure that God is in his camp? At the bottom of this debate, there is only one church which accuses another church. Metaphysical proof is not possible.

But these questions would take us too far afield. They have only one reason for being included here: they make us

NUREMBERG OR THE PROMISED LAND

understand once more and in a somewhat different way that the situation of the victors is tense and precarious, and that injustice is absolutely necessary for them. It is another Dreyfus case. If the defendant is innocent, their world is shaken to its foundation. Let us be on our guard when listening to them, and return to our legal meditations, that is, to this German shoe-maker who was found to be, without knowing it, accessory to a criminal conspiracy after having entered into a legal apparatus which much resembles the deforming mirrors of the Grevin Museum.[14]

To continue, it will be noted that this new manner of conceiving justice revealed a retreat from the Christian world, which is not rigorously Euclidean—it is the Roman world and Roman law which are Euclidean—but this Christian world left open to us the possibility of the opposite sort of correction. In the Christian conception of justice, a man could always plead on the basis of intention. Even if he himself found his actions terrifying: for the phenomenon of optics which plays such an important role in the new law exists also in reality. When the course of events changes direction, our actions can change their appearance, so much so that we can no longer even recognize them. Foreign actions which surround them color their appearance. Acts for which we are not responsible weigh by their proximity on the sector of our own responsibility. What was ourself is then transformed by the play of light and shade and distance in time. A foreigner emerges in the past, and this foreigner is

---

[14] *Grevin Museum* a Parisian wax museum with a Hall of Mirrors (*Palais des Mirages*).

ourself. Christian justice in this respect provided us a right for restitution of our personality; it counteracted the effect of Roman law which is geometrical, scientific, and material. Christian justice knew from experience the existence of this perspective on events, and it gave to man the right to exclaim: "I had not wanted that!" It had even introduced into justice a psychological element which made it possible to oppose to the materiality of facts a psychological materiality which often contradicts them. Human justice had become before all an investigation into causes. It got as close to the action as possible: it leaned over faces. It is enough to point out these principles to see all that we erased with one swipe. Nuremberg does not want to see the faces any more. Nuremberg does not even want to individualize the acts: Nuremberg sees masses, thinks in terms of masses and statistics and delivers us into the arms of a secular justice. One does not judge any more, that is out-of-date: one prunes, one cuts.

This transformation of justice was done with the support of Christians themselves, or at least with that of some of them, and for the greater glory of God. As one perhaps remembers, it was a matter of the defense of the human person. I am not sure that these Christians realized that this regression of the law was an abdication of Christian thought itself, and that by this co-operation they were erasing the patient work of others who had integrated Christ's preachings into Roman law, and that they were reinforcing positions that they did not cease to denounce. These clumsy movements caused by passion and fear have more serious consequences than one might at first think. The Church today has set itself up as a defender of individuals against governments who have done nothing but apply to their own citizens a rule whose universality the Nuremberg judgment had proclaimed. In doing this, the Church sees itself as continuing Christian tradition. But will it not then have to rise up one day against legal equivocations and condemn collective judgments everywhere where they have been given and not only in certain European countries; will it not have to withdraw from the new law issuing from Nuremberg the support which it seemed initially to have given it? It is necessary to make a choice, to speak either like Christ or like Mr. François de Menthon.[15]

It should be recognized however that our jurists have remedies for everything and even for the dangerous life that they now force us to lead. In truth, these remedies are not written in the verdict, they were not revealed at the trial; they arise from the context, from the spirit of Nuremberg, one might say, and finally from the way in which this judgment was presented and commented on. But would our exegesis be complete if we neglected the advice which was lavished on us by authorized spokesmen at the end of the session? These past three years have taught us that the comments of the legal reviewers had no less influence on the destiny of the defendants than the articles registered in the Code.

---

[15] *François de Menthon* a member of the Resistance who after the liberation became Minister of Justice in de Gaulle's provisional government. He was responsible for the trial of Marshal Pétain and for the "purification" of collaborators in the Vichy regime. He was later named by de Gaulle to be prosecutor at Nuremberg. He provided this definition of a "crime against humanity": a "crime against the status of human being, motivated by an ideology which is a crime against the spirit and which aims at throwing humanity back into barbarity."

Look, the scholiasts of our new jurists say, there is a very simple way to tell if the organization to which you belong runs the risk of being declared criminal one day. Essentially, you must mistrust energy. If you catch even a whiff of the adjective **nationalist**, if one invites you to be masters in your own lands, if one speaks to you about unity, discipline, force, grandeur, you cannot deny that that there is not a very democratic vocabulary, and consequently you are likely one day to see your organization become criminal. So, beware of bad thoughts, and know that what we call criminal is always marked out with the same intentions.

The scholiasts agree here with the verdict. The *Judgment* which appears in the first volume of the trial notes the existence of a "plot or concerted plan against peace." This declaration requires many a gloss. But it is clear, in any case, that the plot starts with the existence of the party: it is the party itself which is the instrument of the plot, and, ultimately, it is the plot. This conclusion has some singular consequences. It is actually equivalent to prohibiting people from joining together for the purpose of making certain claims and from using certain other methods for this purpose. What the court means is this: you exposed yourselves to the risk, it says, of one day committing crimes against peace or crimes against humanity, and you cannot claim that you were unaware of this risk since one has written *Mein Kampf* for you. It is thus, ultimately, upon the party's program that condemnation is brought, and accordingly this judgment will constitute in the future an encroachment upon the national sovereignty of every nation. Our jurists say: your government is bad, you are free to change it; but you have the right to change it only while following certain rules. You think that the organization of the world is not perfect: you can try to modify it, but you are forbidden to make recourse to certain principles. However, it may be that the rules that they impose on us are those which perpetuate our impotence or that the principles of which we are prohibited even to think are those which would eliminate the disorder.

This accusation of joining a plot is an excellent invention. The world is from now on democratic for perpetuity. It is democratic by judicial decision. From now on a legal precedent weighs down on every sort of national rebirth. This is infinitely serious, for actually every party is by definition a plot or concerted plan, since every party is an association of men who propose to seize power and to apply their plan which they call a program, or at least to apply most of this plan. The decision of Nuremberg thus consists in making a preliminary selection between the parties. One is legitimate, and the other suspect. Those in the one are in line with the democratic spirit and have the right consequently to seize power and to have a concerted plan because it is certain that their concerted plan will never threaten democracy and peace. Those in the other party, on the contrary, are not entitled to have power, and consequently it is useless that they exist: it is understood that they contain in themselves the seeds of all kinds of crimes against peace and humanity. What is astonishing, moreover, is that the Americans do not understand

Mr. Gottwald's policies:[16] for Mr. Gottwald is doing nothing other than applying in his country the wise precautions suggested by the new Law: he is merely giving the word "democratic" a somewhat peculiar sense.

The right to interfere is therefore inherent in this simple statement. This right, however, is peculiar in that it does not entail, or does not seem to entail, an identifiable will to interfere. It is not some great power in particular or some group of great powers which is opposed to the re-establishment of nationalist movements; it is an entity much vaguer, it is an entelechy without capacities or offices, it is the conscience of humanity. "We do not want to see that again," says the conscience of humanity. What *that* is, as we will see, nobody knows exactly. But this voice of humanity is quite convenient. This anonymous power is only a principle of impotence. It imposes nothing, it does not claim to impose anything. If a movement similar to National-Socialism were established tomorrow, it is certain that the U.N. would not intervene to require its suppression. But the **universal conscience** would approve any government which announced the prohibition of such a party or, for greater convenience, of every party which it accused of resembling National-Socialism. Every national resurrection, every policy of energy or simply of cleanliness, is thus struck with suspicion. They have twisted our consciences and now they look at us limp. Who did that? Who wanted that? It is **Nobody,** just as the Cyclops shouted. The Super-State does

---

[16] *Mr. Gottwald* Klement Gottwald became president of Czechoslovakia in 1948. He nationalized the country's industries, collectivised its farms, and purged many non-Communists (and later Communists) from the government.

not exist, but the vetoes of the Super-State do exist: they are in the verdict of Nuremberg. The Super-State does the evil which it can do, before being able to render services. The evil which it can do is to disarm us against everything, against its enemies as well as against our own.

This is a singular situation. We are disarmed and threatened by an idea and by nothing other than an idea. Nothing is prohibited, but we are warned that a certain **orientation** is not good. We are invited to prepare in ourselves certain sympathies and to instill in ourselves several definite refusals. They teach us how to conjugate verbs, as one does for children: "Mr. Mandel[17] is a great patriot, Mr. Roosevelt is a great citizen of the world, Mr. Jean-Richard Bloch[18] is a great writer, Mr. Benda[19] is a thinker," and conversely: "I will never be a racist, I will like Mr. Kriegel-Valrimont,[20] I will eternally curse the SS, Charles Maurras

---

[17] *Mr. Mandel* Georges Mandel (1885-1944) a French Jewish resistance leader, who was captured in 1940 in Morocco by French forces loyal to Vichy, sentenced to life imprisonment by Marshal Pétain in 1941, and executed in July 1944 in retaliation for the assassination of the Vichy Minister of Propaganda by the Resistance.

[18] *Mr. Jean-Richard Bloch* (1884-1947) a French Jewish Communist writer and militant anti-fascist.

[19] *Mr. Benda* Julien Benda (1867-1956) a French Jewish rationalist philosopher and novelist, who before 1930 had criticized intellectuals for their involvement with politics and nationalism, but who later supported communism, opposed fascism and in particular Nazism, and said that intellectuals "must now take sides."

[20] *Mr. Kriegel-Valrimont* Maurice Kriegel-Valrimont (1914-2006) was a French Jewish militant Communist and a Resistance leader.

and *Je Suis Partout*."²¹ And what about those whose minds are not open to these sympathies, or who reject these refusals? Those whose hearts answer to other calls, those whose minds think only in terms of other categories, those who are made differently? I have the same impression here as when reading certain Marxist texts: these people do not have a brain made like mine, it is another race. This thought puts us back on track. There is a closed world of democratic idealism which is of the same order as the closed world of Marxism. It is not astonishing if their methods manage to coincide, if their justice ends up being the same even though words, as they use them, do not have all the same sense. It too is a religion. It is the same attack on our hearts. When they condemn nationalism, they know well what they are doing. It is the foundation of their Law. They condemn **your truth**, they declare it radically wrong. They condemn our feeling, our roots even, our most profound ways of seeing and feeling. They explain to us why our brain is not made as it should be: we have the brain of barbarians.

This permanent warning prepares for us a form of political life of which we should not be unaware and of which the experience of the last three years on the continent

---

²¹ *Je Suis Partout* (*I Am Everywhere*): the title of a fascist, nationalist and collaborationist journal (1930-1944) to which Charles Maurras was a contributor. Bardèche himself also wrote for it. Maurras was an agnostic anti-Semitic anti-Protestant monarchist Roman Catholic philosopher and writer who rejected much of the teachings in the New Testament. Though a confirmed Germanophobe, he called the German occupation and the subsequent Vichy government a "divine surprise." In September 1944 he was arrested, tried as a collaborator and sentenced to death. The sentence was commuted to life imprisonment. He died shortly after being released in 1952.

does not permit us to be unaware. The condemnation of the National-Socialist Party goes much further than it seems to. In reality, it reaches all the solid forms, all the geological forms of political life. Every nation, every party which urges us to remember our soil, our tradition, our trade, our race is suspect. Whoever claims right of the first occupant and calls to witness things as obvious as the ownership of the city offends against a universal morality which denies the right of the people to write their laws. This applies not just to the Germans, it is all of us who are dispossessed. No one has any more the right to sit down in his field and say: "This ground belongs to me." No one has any more the right to stand up in the city and say: "We are the old ones, we built the houses of this city, anyone who does not want to obey our laws should get out." It is written now that a council of impalpable beings has the capacity to know what occurs in our houses and our cities. Crimes against humanity: this law is good, this one is not good. Civilization has the right to veto.

We lived up to now in a solid universe whose generations had deposited stratifications, one after the other. All was clear: the father was the father, the law was the law, the foreigner was the foreigner. One had the right to say that the law was hard, but it was the law. Today these sure bases of political life are anathema: for these truths constitute the program of a racist party condemned at the court of humanity. In exchange, the foreigner recommends to us a universe according to his dreams. There are no more borders, there are no more cities. From one end to the other of the continent the laws are the same, and also the passports, and also the judges, and also the currencies. Only one police force and only one brain: the senator from

Milwaukee inspects and decides. In return for which, trade is free, at last **trade is free**. We plant some carrots which by chance never sell well, and we buy some hoeing machines which always happen to be very expensive. And we are free to protest, free, infinitely free to write, to vote, to speak in public, provided that we never take measures which can change all that. We are free to get upset and to fight in a universe of wadding. One does not know very well where our freedom ends, where our nationality ends, one does not know very well where what is permitted ends. It is an elastic universe. One does not know any more where one's feet are set, one does not even know any more if one has feet, one feels very light, as if one's body had been lost. But for those who grant us this simple ablation what infinite rewards, what a multitude of tips! This universe which they polish up and try to make look good to us is similar to some palace in Atlantis. There are everywhere small glasswares, columns of false marble, inscriptions, magic fruits. By entering this palace you abdicate your power, in exchange you have the right to touch the golden apples and to read the inscriptions. You are nothing any more, you do not feel any more the weight of your body, you have ceased being a man: you are one of the faithful of the religion of Humanity. At the bottom of the sanctuary there sits a Negro god. You have all the rights, except to speak evil of the god.

* * * * *

The second section of the Bill of Indictment concerns the "crimes against peace."

As is known, the United Nations accuses the German government of having caused the world war by invading

Polish territory, an invasion which forced France and England, in conformity with their commitments, to declare themselves to be in a state of war with Germany. They, moreover, make the German government responsible for the spread of this war because of its aggressions with regard to neutral countries. The charge also claims to establish premeditation by means of two confidential documents discovered in German archives, documents whose authenticity there is little point in denying, given the precautions which were taken for their identification.[22] One is known under the name of the Hossbach Note, the other under the name of the Schmundt File.

The Hossbach Note is the official minutes, written by Hitler's aide-de-camp, of a conference at the chancellery on November 5, 1937, attended by the principal Nazi chiefs; this note is introduced as if it were Hitler's political legacy.[23] It is an exposé, very dramatic moreover, of the theory of *Lebensraum* and its consequences. Hitler there presents Nationalist-Socialist Germany as doomed to asphyxiation

---

[22] Some are less sanguine about the authenticity of the Hossbach Note. Carlos Whitlock Porter in "Documents Used in 'Evidence' at the Nuremberg 'Trial'" (http://www.cwporter.com/document.htm) comments about it thus: "Document 386-PS, the 'Hossbach Protokoll', Hitler's supposed speech of 5 November 1937, is a certified photocopy of a microfilm copy of a re-typed 'certified true copy' prepared by an American, of a re-typed 'certified true copy' prepared by a German, of unauthenticated handwritten notes by Hossbach, of a speech by Hitler, written from memory 5 days later. This is not the worst document, but one of the best, because we know who made one of the copies."

[23] The note itself says that Hitler on this occasion "asked, in the interests of a long term German policy, that his exposition be regarded, in the event of his death, as his last will and testament."

and condemned to find more land. He designates the east as the necessary route for the colonial expansion of the Reich, and he shows that this expansion can be made only by a series of wars of conquest to which Germany is inexorably forced. We will have more to say later about this exposé. If it should be interpreted as the indictment interpreted it—the defendants, however, and in particular Göring, disputed this interpretation—it would constitute proof that Hitler saw and accepted the possibility of war.

The Schmundt File is the official minutes, also written by Hitler's aide-de-camp who at this date was Colonel Schmundt, of a conference at the chancellery on May 23, 1939 at which were present the party chiefs and the heads of Hitler's staff. This conference consisted primarily of a talk by Hitler in which he affirms the inevitability of a war with Poland as the first step in the action of colonial expansion: Hitler considers the consequences of this war and envisages its spreading to the whole of Europe and, by an analysis as dramatic as the preceding one, he makes his generals understand that the coming war will be not a local operation, but will probably be the beginning of a fight to the death with England, of which no one can envisage the outcome. Here too, there are reservations and considerations which spring to mind, and the defense also disputes the scope and thrust of the Schmundt document. With this reservation, the Schmundt File has the same purport as the Hossbach Note of which it represents basically just an application. It would prove in the same way that Hitler was not unaware of the consequences of his policy and accepted the possibility of an European war, while still entertaining the hope that he could avoid one. If these documents were correctly interpreted, it is difficult to maintain that Germany does not carry any share of responsibility for the war.

The accusation also produces a very great number of staff conferences, land maps, and studies of operations of which we cannot here give the details, and in which it also sees evidence of premeditation. As these documents are less sensational than the Hossbach and Schmundt Files and since in addition it is often difficult to distinguish a theoretical and hypothetical tactical study from a plan of operations which one can present as the beginning of an action or as a blatant premeditation, we think that it is enough to inform the reader of the existence of these documents without discussing them.

German historians will have to recognize, moreover, that the German armies were the first to take action: they penetrated into Polish territory, without the German government's having left enough time for the on-going negotiations to develop. They will not fail to point out the bloody Polish provocations which the indictment overlooks and to emphasize the fallacious character of the negotiations which the English cabinet was conducting, it seems, with the hope of seeing them fail; they will also say that the Polish government endeavored to prevent the negotiations and an agreement. These are important circumstances which no assessment of responsibilities for the war should omit and which the Nuremberg Court is certainly wrong not to mention. It is none the less true that it was the German army which fired the first canon shots. On September 1, 1939 a telegram could still have saved everything: this telegram could have come only from Berlin.

This said, here is where the bad faith begins. On one side, one digs through all the files, one probes the walls, one scans the councils, one uses things supposedly said in secret: all is up-to-date, the most secret conversations of the German statesmen are exposed on the evidence table, one did not even forget the phone-tappings. On the other side, silence. One reproaches the German general-staff for studies of operations which were found in their files: you were preparing for war, one tells them. Whom will they make believe that, during the same time, the other European general-staffs were not making a plan, were not preparing to face a strategic crisis? Whom will they make believe that the European statesmen did not act in concert? Whom will they make believe that the drawers of London and Paris were empty and that the German preparations surprised some lambs who thought only of peace? When the defense attorney asked the court to place into evidence similar documents on the French policy for extension of the war, on the English policy for extension of the war, on the maps of the French staff, on the Allies' war crimes, on the instructions given by the English general-staff to their commandos, on the partisans' war in Russia, he was told that that does not interest the court and that the issue raised "is absolutely irrelevant." It is not the United Nations which is on trial, they told them. This answer is quite correct: but then why call **history** what is only a skilful bit of scene lighting? In this case, there is still only half of the earth which has been illuminated. It is on the basis of such appearances that it was formerly denied that the earth was round. History starts when light is spread evenly around, when each one deposits his documents on the table and says: judge. Apart from that, there are only propaganda campaigns. Is it honest to accept this presentation of the facts, was it honorable to mutilate them so? It is more just and ultimately more in conformity with the interests of our own countries to say immediately that this mobilization of the archivists carries no weight with us.

For expertise in scene lighting will not prevail against what is obvious. It is England that declared itself in a state of war with Germany on September 3, 1939, at 11 o'clock in the morning. It is France that made the same statement at 5 o'clock that evening. England and France had legal reasons for making this notification. But, in the end, it is certain that they did it. One is badly placed to reject any responsibility for a war when one was the first to let another state know that one regarded oneself as in a state of war with it. Furthermore, there was in France and in England a war party. They do not hide this from us today. They reproach statesmen for having been at Munich, that is, for having sought a deal (*arrangement*); it is obvious then that they did not want a deal, that they accepted, and even wanted this war. This counts as much as the Hossbach Note, it seems to me. Lastly, everyone knows that after the defeat of Poland, Germany sought to start negotiations on the basis of a *fait accompli*. It was perhaps extremely immoral, but it was still a means of avoiding an European war. These overtures were not accepted. They held on to this war, they decided not to let it go away. There is then lots of evidence a little too strong to be discreetly dismissed. In spite of the play-acting at Nuremberg, the future will easily restore the truth: Hitler agreed to risk a war for a conquest which he considered vital; England decided to impose war on him as the price for this conquest. Hitler thought of starting at most a local military operation; England voluntarily made a world war break out.

One word more is in order before finishing with the discussion of our objections. The indictment devoted much space to the exposition of the aggressions which took place in the course of the war. On this point, if one restricts oneself to noting the **facts**, the position of the indictment is very solid. These aggressions are certain. But does one have the right to present strategic aggressions and the setting off of a world war as though they were acts on exactly the same level, acts of exactly the same gravity? It is assuredly contrary to the law, to justice, and to the treaties, to make an armored division appear at four o'clock in the morning at Copenhagen or Oslo, but is this an act of the same order of magnitude, is this an act of the same essence, as to take the responsibility of setting fire to Europe? Those truly responsible for the war are indirectly responsible to the same degree for the offensive local operations that the unfolding of the war made inevitable. If England had not declared war, Norway would never have been occupied. It is on September 3 that Copenhagen and Oslo started to tremble.

And there still, after reflexion, one cannot prevent oneself from being bothered by certain comparisons. When an English diplomat intrigues to obtain certain economic agreements or tries to obtain or maintain certain political provisions, this is just a free play of influences, it is not aggression, it is not pressuring, it is nothing incorrect with regard to international law: and yet is not this a kind of marking out of the political map, the creation of a zone of influence without military intervention? And when the same diplomat is no longer satisfied to suggest or advise, but abruptly provokes a cabinet crisis which has as a result the dismissal of the germanophile ministers, this too is always the same free play of influences, this too is not called an act of interference: and yet is not this a camouflaged political move-in (*installation*), similar to those interventions for which one now reproaches the Soviet regime? And what guarantee can one have that this political move-in will not prepare, and will not precede, a military move-in? It is so easy to get oneself called to the rescue. The British press, which becomes extremely indignant at these procedures when done by Soviet or German diplomats, always has the tendency to find them extremely natural when they are employed by a British embassy. There is obviously a gap in international law, a gap extremely difficult to fill. But then it is necessary to accept its consequences. The aggressions for which one reproaches Germany (I leave out the attack on Russia) are actually preventive interventions. England did not act otherwise in Syria, for example. In the event of war, weak zones are doomed. A badly defended territory is a prey: it is simply a question of who will be the first to occupy it. The sure solution would be total abstention: that is what the spirit of international law calls for, but the law is, in this area, nearly impossible to apply. Diplomatic methods distort the law; strategic methods ignore it. But it all adds up to the same thing: it is not good to be a strategically interesting neutral.

Thus, in this area where the **facts** appear to overwhelm the German government, one realizes that the reality was not so simple. To present the **facts** without context is a manner of lying. There are no bare **facts**, there are no documents without circumstances: to systematically ignore these circumstances is to disguise the truth. Our lies will not be eternal. Tomorrow the German nation will raise its voice in its turn. And we know already that the world will be constrained to take account of this voice. It will say to us that if Hitler attacked Poland, other men anxiously awaited this attack, desired this attack, prayed that it take place. These men were called Mandel,[24] Churchill, Hore Belisha,[25] Paul Reynaud.[26] The judeo-reactionary alliance wanted "its" war, which was for it a holy war: it knew that only a blatant aggression would enable it to manipulate public opinion.

The German archivists will have hardly any trouble proving to us that the Allied leaders have coldly manipulated the public about the conditions of this aggression. Fear the day when the history of this war will be written. At that moment the context of the local aggressions will appear clearly. The silence of the Allies will then become a self-indictment. It will be seen that they omitted to say that their ploys and their intrigues made the interventions inevitable. Their hypocrisy will appear in full light. And their enormous legal machine will be turned against them because its dishonesty will have been recognized, for he who pours the poison is no less guilty than he who strikes. However, the methods of Nuremberg are a beautiful thing. The absence of any Allied document makes it possible to deny the poison, and international law makes it possible to designate as guilty

---

[24] *Mandel* See note 17 above.

[25] *Hore Belisha* a British Jew whom Neville Chamberlain appointed Secretary of State for War in 1937. He introduced conscription in 1939.

[26] *Paul Reynaud* French prime minister at the time of the beginning of World War II. He had long opposed appeasement and German expansion.

him who is the first to strike. It is the combination of two dishonesties, one bearing on the investigation, the other stemming from the code. With a badly made law and dishonest police officers, we know that one can go far. This truth has been demonstrated to us at our expense.

Thus we have been brought to this first conclusion: that the Nuremberg Trial is not a pure crystal. The National-Socialist plot led to a strong Germany, but this strong Germany did not necessarily lead to war; it asked for the right of live, it asked for it by methods which were irritating, but one could talk with them. Germany was in a permanent state of rebellion against international constraints, it was not in a permanent state of crime against peace. The outbreak of war was due to a combination of circumstances much more complex than the official version admits. Everyone did his share. And everyone had excellent reasons to do so: the U.S.S.R., to think only about it[27] and to want to avoid a trap; England and France, to put a definite stop to German expansion; Germany, to want to break its opponents' smothering policies. And everyone also had ulterior motives and reservations. Would it not be wiser to make a general confession of it? No one is innocent in this affair, and there are things which they definitely do not want to explain: it is much more convenient to have a criminal.

---

[27] *to think only about it* (*de ne penser qu'à elle*) "It" presumably refers to the war. The implication seems to be that the Soviet leaders wished to unite the Russian people in a war effort in order to prevent them from thinking about other things, like the quality of life under Communism. The Italian and German translators take the phrase to mean "to think only about itself," a sense which is grammatically more probable, but seems to me inscrutable in the context.

Our propaganda thus lied by omission and distortion in the assignment of responsibility for the war. In addition, if one traces back from the facts to the principles, one realizes that to make the charges stick we were led to resuscitate a system which had never been able to function and which the facts have condemned many times, in order to support, against experience and the nature of the things, a chimerical and dangerous theory which will confront us in the future with inextricable difficulties. This system has one advantage: it enables us to justify ourselves. But for the sake of offering ourselves this satisfaction, we risk all the mortal consequences of false ideas, for one can falsify history: but reality does not let itself be compelled so easily.

This system is based on the indivisibility of peace and the irrevocability of treaties. It is a kind of geological conception of politics. They suppose that the political world which was in fusion during a certain number of centuries, like the surface of our planet, reached all at once its cooling phase. It reached it by way of a decision by diplomats. The mass of energies is supposed to have solidified; it solidified following certain definite lines of force; this immutable aspect of the political world, this lava flow, from now on fixed and eternal, is what is called the **framework of treaties**. If a fault opens, if a slip occurs somewhere, we must all come to assistance because the whole terrestrial crust is threatened. The history of empires is closed. From now on there is no longer anything but flying teams of rescuers which one calls to do landscaping or shoring up of earthworks.

This solemn stoppage of history which is being generally proclaimed right after a cataclysm: here is what it adds up to in reality. A nation is overcome in a war, one occupies its territory, one plunders its factories, one renders all life impossible for it, then one says to it: just sign this treaty, and we go away, you are on your own, life starts again. This eloquence is persuasive. One always ends up finding a government chief who signs: he covers his head with ashes, he cries, he swears that his hand is forced, he invokes the dark and resounding future as his witness, but he **signs**. From that point, it is finished. Shylock has his pound of flesh. This treaty is without appeal, this treaty is the law. You beseech in vain, you show in vain that these chains render life impossible for you: it is in vain. This treaty has become the definitive basis for your relations to the international community. It obliges not only those who had to sign, but all their posterity. No one has the right to say that he repudiates it. Whoever transgresses it commits a crime. This crime is called a crime against peace. There is not a single violation of the Treaty of Versailles, with which the German leaders were charged, which did not come under this rubric. The Bill of Indictment is expressed as follows: such and such a day of such and such a year, you did such and such an act which was against the Treaty of Versailles, and so on.

Solidified in their irrevocable definition, locked up by force in iron lungs where it is painful to breathe, the vanquished nations implore, they ask to live. It is here where the advantages of geological rigidity appear. One is not inhuman, one listens to them: but one makes them understand that the treaty is for them a bit. Let them be wise, let them admit foreigners in, let them alienate their independence, and this bit could be loosened. One will be able to talk about concessions, perhaps even about revision.

Coffee and oranges in exchange for a democratic government: a Negro a boatload of rice, two Negroes two boatloads of rice, a synagogue a whole convoy. But if they want to be governed in their own way, the law. We choose no other documents to illustrate this situation than the very one which is quoted by the charge, the dramatic conference of November 5, 1937, described in the Hossbach Note. All the deductions of Hitler are based on this dilemma: either we leave power, and then the Anglo-Saxon nations are perhaps ready to consider adjustments to the Treaty of Versailles, which will make it possible for Germany to live, but to live as a tributary; or we remain in power and then our regime is doomed to failure because they will bar us from the raw materials, the outlets and the territories which are for us indispensable. This blackmail is perfectly legal: it is that to which in the end the irrevocable character of treaties leads.

This result is logical, but it is insufficient as experience has proven to us. If one wants to walk quietly on the Sea of Ice, it is necessary to be absolutely sure that no subterranean work is being carried out during this time. Half-submissions create problems. If we want the world to be motionless, this immobility must be controlled. The complete and conscious application of this system should have led us to control German industry, German equipment, the German population, German food, German elections and to exert this control in the name of the nations which solidly support the indivisibility of peace. When one fights life, one should fight it till the end. If you do not want it to take its revenge, the only solution is a racial and economic Malthusianism which one can at most reduce by emigration and export: the vanquished nations will produce goods and slaves for the others. And it will be advisable to supervise them for a very long time by a larval occupation. The Treaty of Versailles condemned us to keep Germany in slavery. It imposed on us, and it imposed on the whole world, a perpetual management which we did not exert. A twenty years long political experiment has forcefully proven to us that for the vanquished there is no middle term between total freedom and servitude.

This however is what the international court refuses to see. Logic frightens it. It lays down premises because they are essential to the accusation, but then it veils its face and does not grant the logical conclusion. It is stubborn like a child, it answers like a child, takes refuge in vagueness, hides behind words. And all that one can draw from the accusers in regard to this very serious issue is this astonishingly vapid and puerile sentence: "It is possible that the Germany of 1920 to 1930 had to face desperate problems, problems which would have justified the most daring measures with the exception of war. All the other methods, persuasion, propaganda, economic competition, diplomacy, were open to an injured nation, but a war of aggression remained proscribed." This is pretty much what we kept telling Germany and Italy for twenty years: Cram yourselves in, make do, but do not come trample on our gardens.

Our Nuremberg jurists thus have not progressed a single step. They wake up from its sleep the old doctrine of the immutable division of the world, they find all the same difficulties with it; and they dare not apply their system strictly. They dare not choose, they cannot choose. If they opt for perpetual servitude of the vanquished, for an avowed and declared servitude, they place themselves into contradiction with all their ideology of war. If they give up trying to prevent by force the breathing and expanding of empires, something which is as powerful, natural and inevitable as the biological laws, they make Germany right and must accept for them the responsibility for the war. This much was obvious, and they knew it: the old diplomacy would probably have tolerated the division of Poland—it was not the first time—and the world war would have been avoided. The annexation of Ethiopia, the disappearance of Czechoslovakia, were they not operations infinitely less expensive for humanity than the outbreak of a world war? That was not right? But the amputation of a quarter of Germany for the benefit of Slavic imperialism, the appalling transfer of millions of human beings whom one has treated for four years like cattle, are these things right? Statesmen formerly knew that one should risk a general war only for infinitely serious causes which put in danger the existence of all nations. And they also knew that it is necessary to make some concessions to the inevitable laws of life. Were we exposed to a mortal danger by the division of Poland? Is not the danger that the democratic statesmen manufactured with their own hands infinitely more grave? Is not our situation infinitely more dramatic? Who today does not think that Europe was beautiful in August 1939? Events have proven Choiseul[28] right. Political forces are natural forces like water and wind: they should be channeled by precise and powerful devices, or it is necessary to navigate by sail. If after wars we

---

[28] *Choiseul* Étienne-François de Choiseul, later the Duke of Choiseul (1719-1785), was a French military officer, diplomat and statesman. He became French Minister of Foreign Affairs in 1758 and essentially controlled French foreign policy until 1770.

do not want to impose servitude which is one of the forms of natural law, it is necessary to accept the alternative, to make viable treaties and to let vigorous peoples develop: the disadvantages which result from their growth are finally much less serious than the start of a general war of which the result benefits only those who threaten our civilization.

Our new jurists, uncomfortable with freedom or servitude, then settled on an intermediate doctrine for which they got some elements from the past and to which they gave a majestic extension. Treaties are irrevocable, peace is indivisible: but, they tell us, do not worry about the appearance of servitude which arises from these proposals, for they are actually the basis of a democratic universe where all nations will enjoy equal rights and the benefits of freedom. Of course, you will be slaves just a tiny little bit , but this is the best means for you all to be free.

To rally support for this clever thesis, the indictment was so worded as to leave the Treaty of Versailles a bit in the shade, for its adversaries referred to it with the naughty word **diktat** and that treaty smacks a bit of the powder of the stronger. The indictment went on to unearth in the diplomatic arsenal a certain number of worn-out pacts which had a very peaceful physiognomy and which were more or less in accord with the idea of free assent. Indeed, our jurists say it is not only the Treaty of Versailles which the Germans violated. They also violated treaties which they had freely signed, the Hague Conventions, the Locarno Pact, the Pact of the League of Nations, the Briand- Kellog Pact. We will not be delayed here by the Hague Conventions: they are vague, at least with regard to aggression. And we have nothing to add to the words of the British prosecutor Sir

Hartley Shawcross: "These first conventions were far from outlawing war or from creating an obligatory form of arbitration. I will certainly not ask the court to declare that any kind of crime was committed in violation of these conventions." But the Locarno Pact and the Briand-Kellog, they repeat to us twenty times: These are something else. These are crowned texts, this is the tabernacle. And the same Sir Hartley Shawcross defines their essential significance by these words: the Locarno Treaty "constituted a general renunciation of war" and the Briand-Kellog Pact constituted another, so serious, so solemn, that starting from this date "the right to make war was no longer part of the essence of sovereignty." Moreover, it is in observance of this pact, adds Sir Hartley Shawcross, that England and France found themselves at war. They did not have to declare war, they were at war, for "a violation of the pact by just one signatory constituted an attack against all the other signatories, and they had the right to treat it as such."

These declarations deserve to be examined closely. One will initially praise them for their subtlety. They are an extremely elegant way of solving the problem of the declaration of war. It is very simple: he who fires off the first canon shot puts himself in a state of war with everyone. Perhaps German historians will ask us why, of all the signatories, England and France were the only ones to show this zeal: we will tell them in response that they are bad spirits and personal enemies of Sir Hartley Shawcross. But that is not all. It is especially on the political level that these proposals are very beautiful and in regard to doctrine very firm: "You agreed, our legal expert essentially said, to belong to a Super-State, you gave up at this point part of your sovereignty, you have no longer the right to go back on this,

this is irrevocable and your signature can be invoked against you." There is much that could be said about this from a historical point of view. Germany withdrew itself from the League of Nations; it was not bound any more by the works and resolutions of the League of Nations. It repudiated the Locarno Pact, which it had renewed once in 1934 for a period of five years, and had not renewed at the expiration of this period: it thus was not bound any more by its commitments at Locarno. It did not repudiate the Briand-Kellog, which moreover contained no clause allowing for its cancellation, but who could have believed himself really bound by Briand-Kellog, since this pact had revealed itself to be inapplicable following the Ethiopian War? That does not matter, says the indictment. These revocations, being unilateral, have no validity for us: Germany, which is no longer part of the League of Nations, is as guilty in our eyes as if it were part of it; the Locarno Treaty has for us as much validity as if it had never been denounced, and the Briand-Kellog Pact, which has no significance when it is a matter having to do with Ethiopia, imperiously obliges Europe to make war when it is a matter having to do with Poland. International pacts have something of a sacerdotal character: they consecrate for eternity.

But it is not the historical aspect of the proceedings which interests us at this moment. Let us admit that Briand-Kellog is a treaty in the same sense as Versailles is a treaty, admit that it was taken seriously by the public and the powers, and admit that this treaty was violated by Germany. What is important, what is a radical change, is the value which suddenly this treaty attains among all the other treaties, there is a sudden promotion, a change of essence which makes of it, not a contract like the others, but a law, a decree by God.

It is here that appears the system which is used as a basis for the indictment, and in particular the unity of this system. In the first section of the Bill of Indictment, the Public Ministry affirmed that there is a universal conscience and an international moral code which are imposed on all men, and that this international moral code prohibited certain forms of political action. Here it affirms that not only the international moral code exists, but that it has instruments, accredited spokesmen, and a legislative power having the same coercive force as the national legislative powers. You did not have the right to make war, says the indictment, because the League of Nations prohibits it: by means of a legislative text at the bottom of which is the signature of your representatives. It is only from this point of view that Briand-Kellog ceases to be a pure declaration affirming that war is a very nasty thing, and becomes an edict prohibiting war. In order for Briand- Kellog to have this value, it must be admitted that the League of Nations was Richelieu: it prohibits war like he prohibited the duel, and it makes Ribbentrop hang just like he had had the head of Montmorency-Boutteville cut off. The League of Nations was thus a power whose constitution Germany violated. England and France, and not only England and France but all the States which recognized the League of Nations, found themselves automatically at war against it, as all the states which constitute the American Confederation would find themselves at war with California if California revolted against the federal power.

Thus the unity and power of the international moral code become perceptible. The universal conscience, or if you prefer, the international moral code becomes a power: it prohibits authoritative nationalism as federal laws prohibit the smuggling of alcohol, and it punishes war like a mutiny. This promotion of the universal conscience enables us to penetrate deeper into the spirit of our new legislators. For them everything holds together, and the second section of the Bill of Indictment is coordinated perfectly with the first.

The attitude of the accusation consists of denying the existence of what exists and affirming the existence of what does not exist. For it, an international moral code exists and has the capacity to make, or not make, written laws which must prevail over the written laws of nations. And, in the same vein, the League of Nations which does not exist any more exists, its policing powers which never existed exist somewhere in the absolute, it is the hand of God, and its regal right exists although it was never affirmed anywhere. This manner of seeing is a form of retroactivity more subtle than the others: for, all in all, the court judges in the name of a Super-State which has a certain existence in 1945 (assuming one believes in the U.N.) but which did not have any in 1939. It is an awakening of phantoms. But above all it is the triumph of the pure essences. All the general ideas begin to have a sword. The clouds make the law. They say that they exist and that only they exist. It is the cave of Plato: our realities are no more than shades, our laws are no more than shades, and the shades say that they are reality and the true laws. It is the triumph of the universals. And we who believe in what exists, we look with stupor at this unleashing of the impalpable.

For finally it must be seen where that leads us. I do not speak here about the shameful use which was made at the Nuremberg Trial of the Briand-Kellog Pact in whose name one claimed to transform into crimes against common law all that the German military had done, under the pretext that, their war being illegal, there were no longer, and there could not be, on their part *acts of war*. I think here of the consequences of this reign of the clouds. The principal one concerns all nations, whether they are, or are not, participants in treaties (for they are all participants in the moral code); it is an abandonment of sovereignty in favor of the international community. This idea is so widespread as a basis for the future world that one invites us every day to accustom ourselves to it. It is so obvious that Litvinov[29] formulated it already twenty years ago as follows: "Absolute sovereignty and entire liberty of action belong only to the states which have not subscribed to international obligations."

How does this relegation of sovereignty come about? Let us note initially that it is not an ordinary abandonment of sovereignty. That sort of thing happens when a nation gives up some of its sovereign rights; for example, it gives to someone else the job of protecting its nationals in the Holy Land, of asserting its rights to manage the Suez Canal, or of regulating the navigation of the Danube. It is not that which is at issue here, we are very far from that. Nations are invited to make this single, incredible resignation: they delegate to a

---

[29] *Litvinov* Maxim Maximovich Litvinov (born: Meir Henoch Mojszewicz Wallach-Finkelstein) (1876- 1951) was a Russian Bolshevik revolutionary and later a Soviet diplomat.

higher authority the right to say what is bearable and what is unbearable, to fix the limit between what they will tolerate and what they will not tolerate, that is to say, they abdicate actually all sovereignty. For what is a sovereign whom one insults, whom one persecutes and who does not have the right to rise and to say: That is enough! Such a sovereign ceases having the character of a sovereign, he becomes exactly a private individual, he reacts as an individual who answers: "Sir, there are courts, there are the courts of the king." He is no longer sovereign since he recognizes a king. The nations thus do not give up part of their sovereignty, they give up their sovereignty itself. Each one of them is nothing more than a citizen of a universal empire. And this situation is so clear that each nation not only accepts some rights, but assumes also some of the duties of citizens. It assumes notably what is strictly speaking *the* civic duty, that which one owes essentially to the suzerain, militia duty. It agrees to be mobilized, it becomes a middle-class citizen (*bourgeois*) of the universe, and it is committed to keep watch in its turn on the order of the council and to follow its commands in general. Each nation is from now on a national guard like the contemporaries of Louis-Philippe.[30]

We see this abdication by nations in its full extent only while remembering what was said in the first section of the Bill of Indictment. For there one sees that the nations give up not only the right to distinguish by themselves what is tolerable and what is intolerable, but they actually delegate

---

[30] *Louis-Philippe* Louis-Philippe of France (1773-1850) was the last French king. He ruled from 1830 to 1848 in what was known as the July Monarchy.

the right to say what is just and what is unjust. It is up to someone else to say not only if they are injured, but if they live in accordance with the moral code. They ask permission for everything, to make war, not to make war, to be strong by such and such a method or to change regime by some other method, to vote for such and such a law or such and such a quota. And it is not astonishing that one now makes **recommendations** to them about their currency, their trade, their budget, their armament, their democratic process; all that was contained in the spirit of Nuremberg and what would be astonishing is if one did not do any of these things.

Thus, the initially sly and purely metaphysical **interference**, when it is a question of our political rights, becomes precise, legal, conditioned by organizations and texts when one passes to the international field. The assimilation of Briand-Kellog to an edict brings out very well the jurisdictional character of the international authority, and the assimilation of states to the condition of citizens brings out very well their degradation. The dramatic transition which we are witnessing has all the characteristics of the phases in which new sovereignties are installed. The same phenomena occurred in Italy of the XVI Century, when the states wanted to impose their legal sovereignty on the feudal princes. Orsini, Malatesta, Colonna claimed to have the right to administer justice in their territories. They could not understand the criminal proceedings that the republic of Venice or the pope took against them, and they died persuaded of their own probity, and were convinced that their enemies had gotten rid of them (which was true) while talking nonsense. One could conclude from this comparison that the Nuremberg Trial is the first demonstration of a new law which will appear obvious in two hundred years. That is possible. But what is even surer is that the Orsini, the Malatesta and the Colonna families disappeared immediately thereafter as sovereigns and that their children became flexible subjects of the pope and the Grand Duke of Tuscany. If Nuremberg determines the law (*droit*) for the future, if international law (*loi*) finally secures for itself the place which is claimed for it currently, our nations will end up like the feudal Italians. These texts consecrate their subjection and their disappearance.

At this point of our analysis we see the panorama of the new system laid out before us. It is in sum a kind of transposition. The irrevocability of treaties and the indivisibility of peace do not lead us to servitude and all its shocking consequences, Malthusianism, control, occupation. But they gently accustom us all to a moderate degree to these phenomena, to a bearable translation of this vocabulary of subjection. It is no longer a matter of "subjection," but of "intervention"; it is not a question of "control" but of "planification," no more a matter of "Malthusianism" but of "organization of exportations," even less a matter of "occupation" but only of "international conferences," which are like medical consultations on our democratic temperature. Everyone is present around the table. Each one has his ballot paper. There are neither conquerors nor conquered. It is freedom which reigns and everyone breathes: not as one breathes in an artificial lung, but as one breathes in the cabin of a bathyscaph or an airship where the oxygen cubage is regulated by a fine intake mechanism. Everyone deposited at the entry a certain number of false ideas and superfluous claims as the Mahometans deposit their Turkish slippers before entering the mosque. Everyone is free because everyone swore before entering that one would eternally respect in his homeland democratic principles, that is, one subscribes eternally and before all else to the Constitution of the United States. Is not this earthly happiness? Is not this a happy compromise between the two difficulties which stopped us a few moments ago? Thus, the squaring of the circle is solved. Germany is condemned not only for having violated the Treaty of Versailles, but principally for having acted contrary to the spirit and the edicts of the universal conscience, that is, of democracy: and it takes again its place among the free nations provided that it swears fidelity to the goddess that it offended.

Only, it is necessary to see these new provisions with all their consequences. This reduction of the states to the condition of private individuals has as its first result to consecrate the present distribution of the world's wealth. Social inequality is reproduced on the level of states, and the same relationship exists with regard to legal institutions. That is, the citizen is named guardian of the inequality which oppresses him. However, in cities this static situation is constantly modified by political struggles. Periodically the citizen lets it be known, and often with a certain violence, that he agrees to continue his role of guardian only if the initial inequality is amended to his profit. The social contract is thus continuously revised. Political action confers on citizens a means of revision; what corresponding means is there on the level of states? Any political struggle at this level is war or a prelude to war, and war, in the new system, can no longer be anything but a world war.

You are free, they tell us, but free with the proviso that you accept your lot. You have rights equal to those of the others, but it should be precisely known that the others gave up the right to call the essentials in question. This is an underhand way to reintroduce Malthusianism. The Charter of the United Nations consolidates pauperism as Briand-Kellog consolidated Versailles. There is not even need of more annexations, there is no need of more coercion, it is enough to make the democratic spirit accepted, for it renders the same service as do all coercions. The rich shout "Hosannah." They give thanks after having sung hymns on the Potomac, and they proclaim that their triumph is the triumph of justice and peace. It is admirable. There is no longer even need to talk of monsters. The monsters have disappeared, it is finished. One does not need to take away their colonies in order to be able to exploit them in their place, or to take away their navy in order to be able to rent them some boats (they have no more boats), or to take away their industry in order to be able to make them buy very expensive pans manufactured in Detroit or manufactured in Essen by the capitalists of Detroit (they have no more factories). It is enough to persuade them to find excellent the present state of things, to look at it as a product of fate against which one can do nothing. The Charter of the United Nations spares the need for a diktat. Versailles is child's play since we have Briand-Kellog. Democracy and immobility, that's our motto; in consideration of which, since all is for the best in the best of worlds, the fleeced are invited to stand guard in front of the inheritance of the just.

Thus, two realms meet and overlap which appeared initially foreign to each other, the moral and the economic. It is peace which Nuremberg claims to guarantee. It so happens that peace and the universal conscience, although they sit in the empyrean, are like kings, about whom Montaigne said that, although they were seated on thrones, they still sat on their asses. Thus, the pure ideas, the impalpable ideas, being incarnated in the place of sovereigns, must use their hands for the impure tasks of the art of the prince. Their administration, in the end, consists in distributing wealth. One cannot take on the administration of the spiritual without jutting out onto the administration of the temporal. One cannot dispossess sovereigns of the spiritual without also dispossessing them of part of the temporal, and that comes with attachments, as the ground comes with roots. So we can say to them: "Pure ideas, impalpable ideas, who then are your ministers? To which attendants, to which chancellors, to which aides did you give the administration of the temporal with which you yourselves do not wish to be bothered? Which congregation reigns on us? If you ask us to stand guard, please let us know in front of what we should stand guard. If you ask us to greet at the door, we would like to know who is seated in your coaches." But the court, in this second section of the Bill of Indictment, does not yet answer this question. It is content to lay down the principles that we described above and through which we seek to read our future.

For we who are surveying the gardens of the new Eden, we see the shapes and the profile of the future world becoming more and more distinct. This new law is definitely a beautiful thing. The first section of the Bill of Indictment drove us out of the city, in practical terms it drove us out, that's a fact; the second section drives out us judicially, by giving us the title of citizen of the world. We learned initially that we did not have any more the right to assemble in the plaza in front of the house of the cadi,[31] and to say: this city belonged to our fathers and it belongs to us, these fields belonged to our fathers and they belong to us. And now that the cadi no more has the right to go preceded by a sword: he has abandoned his sovereignty; now here comes some beautiful agents in white helmets, who announce peace and prosperity. Welcome to you, beautiful agents of our masters! You do not only watch over our sleep, you regulate all kinds of quite different traffics, that of our machines, that of our ideas, that of our money, and soon that of our troops. Our cadi leaves his palace each day to go pray, escorted by his beautiful *goumiers*.[32] He pretends not to see you. And we, returning to ourselves, we think bitterly about the sultans that we used to make parade around like that.

This world that we felt presently to be so fluid, to elude all definition, all certitude, has then at last become somewhat stable, final, irrevocable: it is the laws which render us dependents. In our own places, in our cities, there is no more anything sure, no more certain limits between good and evil, no more ground where to put our feet down: but, above us, what vigorous architecture starts to take shape. A French, German, Spanish, or Italian citizen does not very well know what fate awaits him, but the citizen of the world knows that the harmonious scaffolding of the pacts rises for him. His person is sacred, his goods are sacred, his cost prices are sacred, his profit margins are sacred. The

---

[31] *cadi* an Islamic judge or minor magistrate.

[32] *goumiers* Islamic soldiers or cavalrymen.

universal republic is the republic of merchants. The lottery of history is stopped once and for all. Now there is only one law, that which allows the keeping of what one has gained. All is allowed, except changing places with those on top. The distribution of lots is final. You are a salesman for perpetuity or purchaser for perpetuity, rich or poor forever, master or dependent until the end of times. Where national sovereignties are snuffed out, the global economic dictatorship starts to shine. A people can do nothing any more against the merchants once it has given up the right to say: here the contracts are such and such, the traditions are such and such, and to sit down here you pay such and such a tithe. The United States of the World is only seemingly a political conception: it is actually an economic conception. This motionless world will be nothing more than an enormous commodity exchange: Winnipeg sets the price of wheat, New York that of copper, Pretoria that of gold, Amsterdam that of diamonds. What recourse do we have if we do not agree? A discussion between rich and poor... we know where that leads. A bad mood, the closing of ports? There are thousands of ways to make us regret it. He who gives up the right to tax foreigners, to escort him out of the city with his goods, to close one's ports to missionaries, gives up freedom also and all its benefits. What good is a strike, what good is a social conquest in a country which is forced to align its prices to those of foreigners? This question gives us the key to our present difficulties: one assures the life of his own people only by being master in his own land and by expelling foreigners. But the new "constitution of the world," as President Truman says, invites us to do the very opposite. This policy has a name: for three quarters of a century one called it politely "the open-door policy." We have become China. The election of the president of the

United States is more important for us than our own cabinet crises.

But we have one consolation: the universal conscience which governs us. Perfectly competent lawyers bring us fully made laws. They are the guards of the vestal virgin Democracy. Similar to broad eunuques who supervise the avenues of the harem, they have an unknown face and speak a language which we do not understand. They are the interpreters of the clouds. Their function consists in putting within our reach the invaluable mysteries of freedom, peace, truth: they explain to us what patriotism is, what treason, courage, civic duty consist of. They explain to us our new honor and the face of our new fatherland. O laws of the town, laws of our city, laws full and thick, laws which felt like our flesh and smelled with our odor, laws of our ground! O laws of the prince which the herald shouted out in the boroughs, ordinances about which the counselors voiced their opinions, hat in hand! O old kingdom, time of the corsairs, where are you? O warlike laws, murderous laws, we know it now, you were laws of peace and love! O unjust laws, you were laws of justice! O laws of proscription, you were laws of greeting! O laws of spoliation, you were laws of supervision! O laws, you were our very life and our very breathing. You were the measure of our force, and even in evil our spunk [*élan*] was retained. You were our own blood and you were our soul. You were our face. And we recognized you. Yes, we recognized you: and even the most brutal, even those which we call today unjust, even this revocation of the Edict of Nantes[33] which they teach us to curse, how they appear to us as laws of moderation and wisdom in comparison with the laws of foreigners! Now has come the time of law without a face, the time of falsifications and of murder called law. Today, a machine to manufacture the world has replaced our counselors. From time to time, it puts in circulation a monstrous, dry, hygienic, inhuman product, that we look at with stupor as at a meteorite. And our new legal experts explain us that one could have hung all the German soldiers like ordinary murderers and have shot all French civilians for cooperating with the enemy, but that **one showed indulgence.** O cruel laws of the XIII Century, Custom of Poitou,[34] duel with sticks, *congrès*,[35] judgment of God:[36] today justice and leniency radiate on your faces! Invisible engineers trace out our universe with chalk lines. We had a house, we will have in its place a beautiful sketch. An eye in the middle of a triangle, as on the cover of the catechism, governs the new political creation. The idealists

---

[33] *Edict of Nantes* the edict of King Henry IV in 1598 which granted certain rights to French Protestants known as Huguenots. It also served to keep Roman Catholicism as the established religion of France. It provided no religious rights to non-Christians: hence one is taught to "curse" it today.

[34] *Custom of Poitou* (*Coutume du Poitou*) an edict by Charles VII in 1454 ordering the codification of French law. It was later revised several times.

[35] *congrès* "congress," "sexual union," and by extension (as here) "legal test made in the presence of witnesses (surgeons or matrons) to establish the potency or impotence of the husband when his wife demands for this reason the annulment of the marriage" (*Trésor de la Langue Française informatisé*).

[36] *judgment of God* the euphemistic name for the use of torture, ordeals, forced duels, etc., for the purpose of determining guilt or innocence.

are unchained. All that has given birth to monsters has the right to speak. Our universe will be white like a clinic, silent like a mortuary. This is the century of nightmares. Idealisms, I hate you.

For it is in vain that they take every opportunity to tell us nice things about our independence; that is the simple truth. Today, the victors, thrown into a panic by the consequences of what they have done, can assure us that all that is not so serious, that one will rebuild the cities, that one will distribute coal, machines, gasoline, and cotton—not to the malicious of course, not to the Spanish fascists, for example—that we will have the right to be nationalists as much as we like, hotheads if we want, adversaries of whomever we please, and that nothing has changed: but we know that we are being hoodwinked, and that all the economic plans in the world cannot replace the political rights which they took from us.

Nations have been emasculated. The theory of the United States of the World is an imposture as long as it is founded on a political postulate; the postulate of the excellence of democracy is a postulate exactly similar to that of the excellence of Marxism. And it is also a means of intervention exactly like Marxism. We are no longer free men: and we are not free any more since the Nuremberg Court proclaimed that over and above our national wills there is a universal will which has the only power to write true laws. It is not the Marshall Plan which threatens our independence, it is the principles of Nuremberg. Those who attack the Marshall Plan today do not know it, or do not want to say it, but actually they attack the Nuremberg moral code: half of the French people protest today (without knowing it) because Göring has been hung.

We know, moreover, where that leads. For the convenience of their accusation, the United Nations promulgated an ambiguous doctrine which forces it today to confront some very grave difficulties. Those who believe in the good faith of the Soviets are not wrong. Is not their good faith (in principle) obvious? One asks them to accuse Germany of crime against democracy. On this point, they were in perfect agreement. One proposes to them to promulgate the idea that in the future the world will be governed according to the spirit of democracy. They found that perfectly appropriate. It was only in passing from the principle to its application that one noticed the equivocation. The Russians thought obviously that they had been committed to exporting the Soviet constitution which is, from their point of view, the most democratic in the world; they were completely in favor of interference but by means of communist parties; they wanted many plans, provided that they were triennial, quadrennial, quinquennial; they wanted many exports, provided that they were directed towards the East, and many international conferences if at them they could listen submissively to Mr. Vychinski.[37] They had understood that the democratic spirit was going to blow across the world, departing from Moscow and heading in a counter-clockwise direction. When one explains to them that that wasn't the idea, but that one was

---

[37] *Vychinski* Andrej Jamrjevich Vychinski (1883-1954), Soviet politician and minister.

going to spread the American constitution, diffuse the dollar and the vote with secret ballots, support the inspections of the Red Cross, and meet in the dining room of Mr. Marshall, they declared that there was a serious misunderstanding. Put yourself in their place. They had not made war so that the American ambassador could make it rain or be sunny in Warsaw.

Such is the danger of vague formulas and false ideas. We realize today that the inoffensive Briand-Kellog contained many explosive materials whose existence one did not suspect. It was excellent for condemning Germany, but it is terrible for governing the world. Today the Nuremberg judges, if they want to be self-consistent, must denounce as enemies of the universal conscience the states which in their own lands do not practice democracy in the American manner. They must cut them off from the international community, and the universal conscience, like a suzerain, must make a public proclamation against these rebels. Thus the principles of Nuremberg not only put us under others' supervision, but they condemn us to another war, and to a war very similar to the preceding one, an unnecessary war, an ideological war, a so-called war for what's right. And for this reason thousands of young French and Germans in a few months will perhaps be wearing the same round helmets, in honor of a higher morality which consists, for them and for us, in not being any more masters in our own lands. It is true that in exchange for this policy of Gribouille[38] we will

---

[38] *Gribouille* the name of a proverbial foolish person. The word is used most often in the traditional saying: "Sharp as Gribouille, who throws herself into the water in fear of the rain."

have the satisfaction of knowing that Bolshevism and National-Socialism were two faces of the same monstrosity. I do not know if the Americans saw very well that this additional proclamation would hardly contribute to simplify things.

* * * * *

The third section of the bill of indictment is, like the second, of a very traditional type. It concerns **war crimes**. The court here relies on a precise text: the Hague Conventions of 1907. It calls war crimes acts made by belligerents in violation of these conventions, which regulate the methods which sovereign states have recognized as being in conformity with the laws of war. There is nothing to object to in this process. We will see further on where the dishonesty about this begins. But it was discovered very quickly that the promulgated international law, that is, the text of the Hague Conventions, would not make it possible to reach acts which they wanted to make the Germans pay for. So they invented a new category, as we said, that of **crime against humanity**. And this term was used as the title for the fourth section of the Bill of Indictment. But as no one knew very well where war crimes finished and where crimes against humanity started and since, in addition, it was advantageous to slip into an uncontestable category acts which actually belonged in the contested category, the third and the fourth sections were constantly confused. And it is impossible for us to separate them in our analysis, although the public ministry based these two charges on very different principles.

This part of the Bill of Indictment is that which they fed to the public and let the public ruminate about: we mentioned above why. To judge the seemingly quite reasonable principles to which the accusation made claim, it is necessary first to judge the accusation. And the truth, here, is not as easy to disentangle as one would think. There is an abundant literature on the German atrocities: but this literature is in opposition with what we have all seen. Forty million French men and women saw the Germans for three years in their cities, on their farms, in their houses, on their roads, and they did not find them to be such monsters. Is it we who have been victims of an enormous camouflage under which the Beast was hidden and disguised? And the reports which we were given, were they not exaggerated? We derive no benefit from defending "good Germany": for the policy of the French government during the occupation appears much more effective if the Germans are indeed monsters. The resistants, on the contrary, may find it beneficial to display their sufferings: one knows well enough that sufferings are easily transformed into plazas.[39] Were we mistaken about the Germans? We are ready to recognize this in good faith, we would not be diminished by it: but is it true?

That is the first difficulty. There are others which are combined with this one. They accuse Germany of the extermination of a large number of human beings. Quite understandable, we condemn such proceedings at any time,

---

[39] Plazas and public squares in France are frequently named after martyrs of the Resistance.

even in time of war. This point has never been in question for any of us; and if during the war we had known about certain acts for which one reproaches Germany today, we would have protested against these acts. But we repeat: we must first require an impartial verification of these charges, a verification which has not yet been made; and secondly, we cannot discuss these things while pretending to forget that the Allies undertook on their part, by different but just as effective methods, a system of extermination almost as widespread; and finally, we French, we are not permitted to be unaware, in expressing our judgment, that this extermination (the accusation itself makes this clear) would have been directed especially against populations which one can call alien, mainly against Slavs. The propaganda by the Resistance aimed to confuse everything: it talked about the concentration camps as if the French had been treated like the Slavs, and it chose everywhere the biggest atrocity and presented it as the rule. The result is that the readers of our newspapers are convinced that every day in Ravensbrück they threw five hundred Belleville children into furnaces while singing *Lili-Marleen*.[40] We have thus also to exercize some restraint on this point. We recognize that an appalling toll of life was taken in the conflict between Germany and Soviet Russia: and, at the risk of surprising many readers, I will add that if one regards as correct the figures of the Russians' losses and sufferings presented by their government, the Russians would seem to have been

---

[40] *Lili-Marleen* a German love song about a soldier on guard duty. According to Gordon Brock, it was "surely the favourite song of soldiers during World War II, Lili Marleen became the unofficial anthem of the foot soldiers of both forces in the war" (http://ingeb.org/garb/lmarleen.html).

moderate in their reprisals during the occupation. If it is true that their prisoners were massacred by the hundreds of thousands, that their districts were destroyed, depopulated and razed, that their peasants were hung in bunches; if what they affirm turns out to be true, they would have had the right, under the terms of the law of retaliation which we cite so often, to transform half of Germany into a charred desert: but they did not do this, they had the cool-headedness to understand that the removal of their intractable enemies and the installation of a regime under their control were more important objectives for them than revenge. And they let us juridically condemn the Germans for deeds which their politics led them to wipe away. Let us not then show ourselves to be more royalist than the king. What occurred in Auschwitz, in Majdanek, and other places concerns the Slavs: we, we have to concern ourselves with the Occident. Let us not claim those debts which the debtor does not pursue. But let us take care to rectify here the excesses of our own propaganda. What is important for us is to know what the Germans have done **to us**. It is on this point that we will question the documents of Nuremberg.

This task is all the more easy since, with regard to the Western sector, it is to the French Public Ministry that the court has entrusted the job of presenting the acts deemed to be war crimes and crimes against humanity. We thus have thereby an excellent means of surmounting the first of the difficulties which arose a few moments ago. This official indictment enables us to neglect the private indictments gathered by impromptu journalists or writers, which the French prosecutor did not judge suitable to retain. And, at the same time, it enables us easily to isolate what is related to our country among all the charges formulated pell-mell against National-Socialism. Our goal is thus to ask ourselves first: the German atrocities, about which one reads recollections every day in our press, have they been proven? And the most solemn of our complaints, the only authentic one, that which was expounded at Nuremberg, what proofs support it? Instead of going on immediately to the examination of principles and instead of sitting down near the judge and watching him judge, it is necessary first here to look into the evidence cited; it is necessary to try to see what is solid in the indictment. We are going, with the court, to listen to the witnesses and to smell the exhibits. And, then, we will ask: And you?

It is enough to read, even quickly, the transcript of the Nuremberg Trial to perceive that from the moment when the French delegation, to whom this part of the indictment was entrusted, rises to articulate its charges, the methods of the trial are completely transformed. The American and English delegations, whose job it was to support the first and the second sections of the Act of Indictment, had respected a certain number of rules, which were not obligatory in terms of the regulations of the International Court, but which were quite prudent. For example, the majority of the quoted documents were German documents found in German archives and signed by identified persons in charge: it happened sometimes that the Public Ministry deposited a document coming from one of the Allied states, but if they did this, they declared it expressly, with the implication that these documents did not have exactly the same value as the documents of German origin. In the same way, the witnesses quoted up to now, with maybe one exception, were German civil servants or generals, Colonel Lahousen of the staff of General Canaris, the General Ohlendorf of the SS, Major

Wisliceny, Eichmann's assistant for the handling of Jewish questions, General Schellenberg of the SS, the guard Hollrieg from the camp at Mauthausen, General von dem Bach Zelewski of the SS, the submarine officers Heisig and Mohle. Objections from the defense about the origin of documents were rare; the president almost never had to arbitrate incidents. From the moment when our delegate rises, all that will change, and the bases for the accusation appear so different, they create so many incidents, they cause so many interventions from the Court itself, that it is impossible to consider this indictment without subjecting it to a preliminary analysis.

The first anomaly is the almost total disappearance of German documents and testimonies. It cannot be said that this disappearance is indifferent. It is serious: the French prosecutor is not there to enumerate "crimes of Germany," for one cannot hang "Germany," but he claims to prove that these crimes are the result of orders given by the men who are in front of him and whom he accuses. He asks that one inflict the death penalty on Keitel, whose general district was somewhere on the Dnieper,[41] on von Neurath who was Reichsprotector of Czechoslovakia, on Ribbentrop who was a Foreign Minister, on Speer who was in charge of armaments, on Jodl who directed the military operations, on Baldur von Schirach; and he provides no document proving that Keitel, Neurath, Ribbentrop, Speer, Jodl, etc., ordered the crimes, perhaps real, that he describes. He lightly asks for

---

[41] *Dnieper* a long river which begins west of Moscow and flows south through Belarus and Ukraine and empties into the Black Sea.

these human lives although he has no evidence. In a pinch he can well assume that Göring **knew** (Göring claimed the opposite) or, in any case, that he **should have known**; he is right perhaps to affirm that Kaltenbrunner, Himmler's assistant, and Seyss-Inquart, the Governor of Holland, **could not not have known**, and that that follows from the very nature of the offices they held, but that proves neither the existence of a plan, nor the execution of personal orders from the defendants. In a lawsuit against Germany, he could well say that it is necessary for him to resort to the testimony of victims and that it is impossible to do differently: but this is the first dishonesty: he is not prosecuting a lawsuit against Germany, he would very well like to do that, but he is not doing it. The entity called Germany was not convened by the usher; he speaks against men, seated in front of him, convened to answer for their acts and not the acts of others, and he does not have the right to affirm the existence of a concerted plan to destroy the French population, since he cannot prove it, nor does he have the right to accuse men of having given orders which he cannot establish to have existed.

The second dishonesty of the French delegation consisted in replacing the evidence that they did not have and the orders that they did not have (and about which it was incorrect to say in front of a court that they existed since they were not provided) by an enumeration. I will not provide evidence, said the French delegate, but I will make appear so many witnesses, I will deposit so many reports, that it will be the same thing as a proof, for one will see that everything happened in the same way everywhere, all of which presupposes orders. Beautiful thing to say in the country of Descartes! The fourteen years old boys, in our high schools, are told that the first rule of the scientific method is indeed to be based on **complete** enumerations. This small adjective is essential, for in this small adjective lies honesty. However, the French delegation (in this it acted like French courts of justice) detests complete enumerations. The French delegation confuses enumeration and sample. It picks out some police reports which talk of massacres, and it concludes: one massacred everywhere; Mr. Keitel, within your general district on the Dnieper, you gave **the order** to massacre in Annevoye, in Rodez, in Tavaux, and in Montpezat de Quercy. It makes appear three or four deportees who describe their concentration camps, and it concludes: things were similar in all the concentration camps, and that well proves, that there was everywhere in all of you, in you Speer, in you Dönitz, in you Hess, and in you Rosenberg, a **systematic will** to exterminate. I expose, therefore I prove. I show photographs: it is as if you had been everywhere. I complain, I ask for revenge, and this complaint must have for you the same value as a legal proof: all the more so as these are "resistants" whom you have the honor to hear. The French delegation believes itself to be before the Court of Justice of the Seine,[42] and it does not understand when the president interrupts rather coldly.

However, the documents with which the French delegation replaces evidence are due to the same optical error, and it is that which is so embarrassing for this whole part of the trial. Sometimes the French delegation harps on

---

[42] *Court of Justice of the Seine* This court condemned to death many resistants during the war and many collaborators after the war.

particular incidents which, however painful they are in themselves, have no general significance at all: thus the arrest of General Giraud's family, about which there would be much to say, by no means proves that the families of resistants were systematically deported to Germany, and we all know that that is nonsense. Good statistics would have made the point better. Sometimes, they brandish small pieces of paper that they sniff, examine, hold up to the light and look over and through, all the while seeming very suspicious: there is the senior police officer of Saint-Gingolf (Var) who certifies something about the administrative internments, there is the Military Security of Vaucluse which assures us that life was unpleasant in prison, there is the chief of staff of the F.F.I.[43] who found an instrument with balls.[44] For those which know that the majority of the impromptu police officers at the time of the liberation had to be demoted later, that a certain number of the members of the Military Security are now incarcerated, and that the chiefs of staff of the F.F.I. had often gained their stripes only the day before, these over-stuffed "reports" are not very impressive. A serious investigation would have revealed that the staff varied from prison to prison, that one could be locked up in Fresnes and not be tortured, that certain police forces behaved correctly and that others were composed of torturers, that even the methods of the Gestapo in France varied according to the subordinates who were in charge. So,

---

[43] *F.F.I.* = *Forces françaises de l'intérieur*, French Forces of the Interior. This is the title given by the Allies in 1944 to the Resistance fighters within France who were ready to support an Allied invasion.

[44] *an instrument with balls* presumably an instrument of torture.

the president was not wrong, when confronted with the singular proceedings of this investigation, to sigh, to interrupt, and finally to admit these reports only after stating his reservations about their "convincing value," and apparently because he understood that, by rejecting them, he would have reduced the French delegation to silence.

But it is in reports (*dans le récit*) that the French delegation shines the most. One feels a certain embarrassment here to say all that one thinks: for he who wonders about the exactitude of the facts and the probity of the witnesses while one tells him the report of others' suffering exposes himself to the reproach that he lacks heart and even that he is inaccessible to the simplest human feeling. But it is impossible not to say that reports told by non-eyewitnesses who heard them from non-eyewitnesses, reports moreover which have been spread around and are necessarily presented without their accompanying circumstances, all in all constitute only a means of arousing emotion; but in no case do they replace a serious and complete investigation of the behavior of the German army in France. These are only isolated instances; and as such, it is possible that they implicate the responsibility of local officers, but one cannot claim to present the history of the military occupation of France between 1940 and 1944 by means of twelve reports of tortures or reprisals, all of which take place in 1944 and in areas where there was a sniper at the corner of each small wood. About such matters it is necessary to say nothing or it is necessary to say everything. A partial account is a biased account (*Un récit partiel est un récit partial*). About this one day they will tell us: France lied.

The methods which we describe however constitute a system in the presentation by the French delegation. They believe they are in front of a jury. One asks them for a report (*rapport*), they prefer an exposition. They dedicate themselves to the exposure of German crimes: the more horrid, the more the delegation triumphs. Oradour-sur-Glane, Maillé, Tulle, Ascq, it is no longer a magistrate who speaks, one would say it is rather the press of September 1944. It is no longer a question of dispensing justice, the whole point is simply to denigrate the enemy. The French delegation agrees to take part, it burns to take part, by an official demonstration, in this enterprise of denigration and hatred that the most ignoble press of our history displays in front of the public. Conscience and honor on the part of magistrates, that's just archaeology for them: they have become journalists. And these men, whom we have had to watch (painfully and despite ourselves) represent our country, do not even understand that there is something revolting in these courteous and cold interruptions by the president who reminds them in his own way, that even in such a court as this there is a minimum of propriety.

This dishonest presentation, this constant appeal to the lowest instincts of the public led them, moreover, to miss their goal completely. What one asked for, what one had the right to ask for from the French delegation, was an objective and useful report about the German occupation of the Western countries between 1940 and 1944. No serious person will agree to say that such a report appears in the official indictment at the trial. The question of economic plundering is the only one treated conscientiously and the only one presented with figures which could be used as a basis for a discussion. For the rest, there is no general picture, no statistics, no effort to put things in order and to present information honestly. In ten years time, a German historian will have no trouble to take up the report of our representative and to comment on it with documents, dates and figures, in order to lambast us with an implacable demonstration of our bad faith. He will easily show that German policy, even with regard to the police force and the army, was different in 1941 and in 1943, that certain German administrative authorities protected as far as they could French lives and that finally, as everyone knows, the life of the French people was bearable at least until the beginning of the year 1944. He will tell us that there are confusions which one does not have the right to voluntarily create, when it is a question of accusing men, even if one thinks that these men are monsters. He will prove to us that the plan for the extermination of the French people never existed, which explains extremely well why one found no trace of it, and that, consequently, we did not have the right to make accusations under this rubric against men like Keitel and Jodl, simply because we had the misfortune of not having been able to find Himmler alive. He will explain to us why this policy of substitution of responsibilities, which we put to so much use with regard to our compatriots, is a legal comedy which dishonors those who employ it. The facts show us (unfortunately all too easily) what a policy of extermination is. For in the transcript of this same trial, only a few pages away from the French exposé, there is an exposé which crushes us: it is that of the Soviet delegation. Yes, in the East of Europe, there is a terrible score to be settled between Germany and its neighbors. Yes, there, there was a policy of extermination. And, there, one found traces of it. Not by an **enumeration**, our favorite method. Not by **samples**. One found the plans for it in the Führer's conferences, one found the instructions for the persons in charge, one found orders, one found everything. This alarming policy seems to have been carried out unfortunately; at least there are documents which say so. And if we share at all the hypocritical pain of the indicters of Germany, it is by our sincere pain while thinking of these men and these women of Ukraine who received the Germans with flowers as though their coming meant salvation and the right to live, and who were massacred, famished, exterminated, stupidly, by these men whom they received with cheers and who had perhaps in their pocket the order to make them disappear. That, yes, that is a crime. But is it true? There are all sorts of things in these documents, and they were not always classified with prudence. One presented several times as orders discussions which were only memoranda, that is, suggestions which were rightly rejected. Other times, one showed orders, but it turned out, in the course of the trial itself, that these orders were not carried out by the army commanders who found them too severe. Other times, one was mistaken about the meaning of certain measures; for example, the systematic destruction of villages was not a policy of terrorism, but a means of fighting partisans, which consisted in evacuating the cattle, then the inhabitants, and finally in destroying the dwellings themselves, so as to create around the partisans a kind of "burned earth," similar to that which the Russian command itself had created around German divisions. In the same way, destruction of buildings or harvests, raids on the populace were employed by the two armies, the Russian army in its retreat and the German army in its retreat. The Germans have even asserted that they had done an immense amount of construction in Ukraine, that they often had helped and supplied the population, which is the exact opposite of what one tells them. Whom then ought one to believe? The figures presented by the Russian delegation are unverifiable. What if the Russian delegation had used the Nuremberg Trial for an enormous display of propaganda, like the French delegation? We can check on what the French delegation says, that occurred in our own lands. But who can check on what the Soviet delegation says? On this point, the trial is open: and we would be very wrong to believe it settled by the verdict.

But, even taking into account propaganda and falsification, even without taking a position about the most basic elements of this report since we cannot, who does not see that the figures and the facts alleged by the Soviet delegation overwhelm us? The French delegation would well have spared itself some odious and shameful procedures, if it had reflected that its exposé would be printed only a few pages away from this terrible file. And it would have been well advised not to make it possible for the reader to confront the figures for the so-called will to exterminate the French people with the figures which depict the extermination of Slavic peoples. It is sad, certainly, to have to count our victims: 77 in Ascq, 120 in Tulle, 800 in Oradour, and to have to cite 6 villages burned in France, 12 in the Belgian Ardennes. But, even with these facts, one does not speak of a will to exterminate, when a Soviet prosecutor can rise and cite 135,000 shot in the area of Smolensk, 172,000 in the area of Leningrad, 195,000 in Karkhov, 100,000 in Babi-Yar, close to Kiev, and affirm that the German army destroyed 70,000 villages. Even if the Soviet prosecutor distorted or exaggerated the facts, this simple juxtaposition proves that the orders for extermination which one seeks for France never existed, and that there existed, on the contrary, instructions prescribing a policy of considerate treatment. It would have been honest to recognize that. If anything justifies our policy of reason and sang-froid with Germany during the years of occupation, it is this indicator of what would have awaited us if we had done otherwise.

But let us leave this digression, and come back to the French delegation. It sometimes happens that it finds evidence, this French delegation, or at least that it claims to find some. It would like to act like everyone else, the French delegation, and from time to time proudly deposit for the court, on the president's desk, a document written in German. Unfortunately, when one undertakes to prove something which does not exist, initially one hardly finds documents, and then with the documents which one finds, it happens that there are disappointments. These two peculiarities characterize the French documentation. Initially it is rare, and one can say about it, as about the prescriptions of Doctor Knock,[45] that one could not create a big volume by gathering together the German texts which are in it. And then, there is always something lame in it, it is in contradiction with what someone said, it is not signed, it is not clear, and, alongside the documentation of the other delegations, in truth, it looks pretty sad.

If the French delegation succeeds in discovering an order concerning tortures to be applied in interrogations, one realizes in examining it that this order precisely prohibits the sort of tortures which had just been alleged, and limits to

---

[45] *Doctor Knock* a quack doctor who is the main character in Jules Romains' satirical play, *Knock*.

some very precise cases the use of certain means of coercion, all well defined: that does not prove that German police officers did not torture, but it does certainly prove that one had not given them orders to torture, as is the case moreover with all the police forces of the world. If the French delegation finds some invoices for harmful gas, it makes a mistake in translation; it says there is a sentence where one can read that this gas was intended for "the extermination," whereas the German text actually says that it was intended for "the cleansing," that is, for destruction of lice, about which all the internees themselves in fact complained: and in addition, in examining these invoices, one realizes that some of them are intended for camps which never had gas chambers. The French delegation intrepidly neglects this detail and connects these famous invoices to a phrase which one of the witnesses says he heard from the mouth of a German warrant officer at the time of his arrest. This arbitrary connection does not shock it a moment, and it considers that with a bundle of inaccurately interpreted invoices and a phrase drawn from thin air, it "amply establishes" this "will to exterminate," so obstinately sought.

If it finally manages to deposit an authentic document, it draws an abusive interpretation from it. It cites, after many others, the famous decree *Nacht und Nebel*,[46] but since Hitler is not there to take the responsibility for it, it quietly

---

[46] *Nacht und Nebel* (*Night and Fog*), a directive signed by Hitler on Dec. 7, 1941 and implemented thereafter by Chief of Staff of the Armed Forces Wilhelm Keitel, which revised and greatly harshened Germany's treatment of political prisoners in the occupied territories. In brief, it meant that they would no longer be treated in accordance with the Geneva Conventions.

attributes it to Keitel who had protested against this decree. It cites, likewise after some other delegations, a document on the lynching of Allied aviators, but it forgets to say that this document was only a plan and that it never became an order or an instruction because the military authorities were opposed to it. And all is of the same soundness. There is always something to correct in these productions, which the defense does not fail to correct—and even sometimes the president on his own initiative. The famous will to exterminate appears to the French delegation "established" by a letter "which was not yet authenticated," and which besides applies only to Jews. The French delegation reproaches the German military authorities for having refused repatriations of prisoners wrongly captured after the signature of the armistice: it takes note of a letter of Ambassador Scapini of April 1941, but it forgets to say that on this date the German army had released spontaneously or after negotiations several hundred thousand French prisoners. It produces a witness of the penal camps for escaped prisoners: these penal camps were very harsh, but it would have been honest to say that, generally, the 900,000 French prisoners who were in the hands of the Germans during the war were treated in accordance with the Geneva Convention.

Errors by omission, by inaccuracy, by distortion of responsibilities, by carelessness, by interpretation, these are what one constantly finds in the file deposited by the French delegation. If one discovers so many blunders in this official documentation, if one never has the impression of honesty, of an absolute trustworthiness on the part of the men who were assigned to speak in the name of our country, then what is the file worth? What is the investigation worth? And what protects us from a charge of falsification?

But that is not all. There are still our witnesses. These witnesses, they are of the same order as the reports and expositions. As we know, the French delegation had a copious supply of witnesses. Let us repeat it once again: it was not a matter of judging just Kaltenbrunner, Himmler's assistant, but also Jodl, Keitel, Ribbentrop, Dönitz, and Hess, etc. But the French delegation does not address itself to the Court: the French delegation addresses itself to humanity. Let us see then by whom it lets itself be represented before humanity. We mentioned above who had been the witnesses of the American and English Public Ministries. Perhaps these German witnesses did not tell the whole truth: for they were thinking of their own trials; it could have been useful for them to accuse their chiefs. But at least, to a future German historian, one could say that these witnesses had deposed without hatred, without intention to harm. The witnesses of the French delegation are of another nature. For them a German is the enemy; he will never be accused enough; they are there to describe atrocities, to give a talk about the atrocities which they saw, about those that someone told them, and about those that someone told their friends; the only problem for them is not to show this hatred too much, to keep, at least in their presentation, an appearance of objectivity.

The parade of these witnesses, moreover, fills the reader with a certain stupor. One would not have believed that thoughtlessness could go so far. The first testimony which they present at the court is an affidavit by a woman, Jacob. It concerns the camp of Compiegne and begins as follows: "We were visited by several German personalities: Stülpnagel,[47] du Paty de Clam[48]... " That made one prejudge the rest. One sees appear successively some personalities of the same mould. There is Marie-Claude Valiant- Couturier, Communist deputy, and after her, a witness named Veith, another named Boix, another named Balachowsky. Their interrogation starts as follows: "*The President.* – Would you sit down, would you spell your name, please? – *Mr. Veith.* – Jean-Frederic Veith. I was born on April 28, 1903 in Moscow." To the next one: "*The President.* – What is your name? – *Mr. François Boix.* – François Boix. – *The President.* – Are you French? – *Mr. Boix.* – I am a Spanish refugee." And one learns that Mr. Boix was born in 1920 in Barcelona. To the last one: "*The President.* – What is your name? – *Dr. Alfred Balachowsky.* – Balachowsky, Alfred. – *The President.* – Are you French? – *Dr. Balachowsky* – French." And a few moments later: "*Mr. Dubost (representative of the French Public Ministry).* – You are

---

[47] *Stülpnagel* Karl-Heinrich Rudolf Wilhelm von Stülpnagel, a German general who was in charge of France from February 1942 to July 1944. He had little sympathy for Hitler's racial tenets, was involved in the plot to assassinate Hitler on July 20, 1944 and, when it failed, was arrested and later executed. The mention of the visits by Stülpnagel and du Paty de Clam is ironic and undercuts the point that the speaker wishes to make, for these two men were known to be sympathetic to the prisoners' plight and would have visited the camps precisely in order to see that prisoners in them were not being mistreated.

[48] *du Paty de Clam* Charles du Paty de Clam was Vichy's Commissioner General for Jewish Affairs. Despite the fact that his father Armand had been Dreyfus' chief accuser, he was only mildly anti-Semitic and took this position with the approval of the Resistance, in order to be able to undermine Vichy's persecution of the Jews. He was condemned and imprisoned after the war, but was pardoned after his relations with the Resistance were corroborated.

staying in Viroflay? You were born on August 15, 1909 in Korotchla in Russia? – Dr. *Balachowsky* – That is correct." And that's it. In all, of nine testimonies presented by the French delegation, only three, those of Mr. Lampe, Mr. Dupont and Mr. Roser, are testimonies of men born on French ground. I do not include here the testimony of Marie-Claude Valiant-Couturier, a Communist deputy, which was obviously dictated to her by her party, as well as the speeches that she gave to the Chamber, and which, by her exaggerations on the most tragic of subjects, provoked outbursts of laughter that the president had to calm by his intervention.

Thus, among our nine testimonies, there were a certain number of depositions which we made **suspect** by the mere mention of the civil status of the witnesses. Can one maintain at least that the other depositions are unattackable? It is possible, and in the absence of a contradictory investigation that no one has yet had the possibility to make, one must admit that they have, temporarily, a certain authority. Still, they should be examined with the means we have. Of these three testimonies, two are testimonies of deportees: one of these was deported to Mauthausen, the other to Buchenwald. However, these two witnesses were deported respectively, one in March 1944 and the other in January 1944. Even supposing that one regards their testimony as indisputable, it remains that this testimony can be first-hand only for the period following their internment. Was it not useful to check by means of other testimonies if the administration at Mauthausen and that at Buchenwald had been the same during the previous years? The third witness is a warrant officer, a prisoner of war, who escaped nine times and was nine times recaptured and who bears witness about the disciplinary camps for prisoners of war. Whatever the confidence which his testimony inspires, the Public Ministry was at fault in its handling of it: for they let him testify imprudently on facts which he did not see, which comrades told to him or which were told to his comrades. That gives the following result: "A soldier whose name he has forgotten" told him "in a city whose name he has also forgotten" on a date that he cannot specify, etc. Such and such important information was given to him "by a kitchen-worker," and it is awkward for this information that it is contradicted by documents which one found elsewhere. As one can imagine, the defense has no trouble in triumphing over this second-hand and third- hand testimony: one lawyer even succeeds, not without some malice, to make the witness describe an assassination which he had stated a few minutes earlier not to have been present at. Of course, this does not mean that there were no disciplinary camps, that there were no assassinations of escaped prisoners, that there were no concentration camps. But on matters so serious was it not preferable that the documents poured out by the representatives of France be undeniable and especially that they be complete? Our witnesses hardly control their hatred, they shout, as in front of our Courts of Justice, that they have comrades to avenge, they affirm that they will not allow this to be forgotten, that they are there for that. Only, we, we ask them for the truth: it is not the same thing. When the defense questions them in its turn, one then sees them put on a singular spectacle. The defense, for them, is obviously the enemy. It is a question of not letting themselves be taken in its traps. They become flexible like Proteus, twisted like Pathelin:[49] they answer but not to the point, they do not answer, they are on their guard above all else not to let the defense have any advantage, they are the witnesses of the Public Ministry. Because they came there as accusers, they are the loudspeakers of the Resistance and of the Resistance's propaganda; they are not, they are not at any time men who have come from their city to help the court establish the truth.

This objection is grave. It is grave because it is accompanied by all kinds of circumstances which it is necessary to have the courage to mention. And initially it is impossible not to ask oneself, in certain parts of these depositions, if it is not a question of coached testimonies. There are answers, there are assertions, which are not like direct testimony, and which come back like refrains. One questions the witnesses about the famous "will to exterminate" the French people. Without any doubt, they answer in chorus, there was a will to exterminate; without any doubt, there were "higher orders." One questions them on the responsibility of the entire German people. Without any doubt, they affirm in unison, the German people knew what occurred in the camps. One questions them on the membership of the guard services of the camp. They are always SS, they declare without failure. The cross-examination reveals in vain some surprising things, that the Jews were immediately put aside, that it was forbidden to the

---

[49] *Pathelin* Pierre Pathelin, a shady lawyer in the medieval satirical play, *The Farce of Master Pathelin*, written around 1460.

German guards, under penalty of death, to speak about the camps, that the SS were sent to the front after 1943 and were replaced by locals of some sort, that does not change anything. The witnesses pronounce with certainty on questions which they are not in position to answer with certainty, and they answer precisely what the French delegation needs to hear said.

There are circumstances even more troubling. Why did one make these witnesses depose, and them only? Since they have affirmed to us that one could support the charge only by a sampling, what principle governed this selection? Did one want to give an accurate idea of the German occupation and of the internment camps, or did one seek, above all, witnesses for effect? Why do all the testimonies cover the year 1944? Why do they concern only the camps at Mauthausen and Buchenwald, whereas there were twenty internment camps and two hundred commandos?[50] It is recognized that among the deportees there were a certain number who had been interned because of involvement in the black market or for common crimes. Why do they not specify the percentage of these? Why was no internee of this category heard? They explain to us that the *kapos* selected by the Germans from among the internees were responsible for most of the atrocities which were committed. Why were none of the internees who accepted this role convened? Everyone knows one of them, at least in our country, and this business created quite a stir. There are several hundred others of them. The history of the camps thus was not so

---

[50] *commandos* camps for prisoners of war.

clear, and there are things which one prefers to leave in the shade? But then, if one does not tell us all, what are they worth, this prefabricated history and this factitious sampling? However, of this preliminary filtering of testimonies, we have evidence, we are starting to have evidence. Some prisoner of war was convened by a board of inquiry for the gathering of testimonies. He told what had happened to him during his captivity. He was thanked, and it was explained to him that his testimony was not retained because it did not contain any weighty element against the Germans. Another deportee was approached too. He was in Mauthausen like the witnesses for the prosecution. He does not speak about Mauthausen exactly in the same way. He was convened. His testimony was recorded. But they did not use it, without explaining why to him. It is clear that one did not try to have counterbalancing testimonies on this question. I come to a rather strange circumstance which is of the same order. It was reported in an investigation by the Spanish weekly magazine *Madrid*, and it was confirmed to me besides by several correspondents. Why would we refuse this testimony since Mr. Dubost admits that of Mr. Boix? It is about the enterprise of camouflage and re-construction pursued by the victors for the purpose of creating a kind of promotional tourism. In order to set off people's imaginations, one has transformed a certain number of camps into museums. It is thus by means of wax mannequins, restored gas chambers, and scenes of torture made up as at the Grévin Museum,[51] that one preserves the memory of the horrors described by propaganda. That's

---

[51] *Grévin Museum* See note 14 above.

okay up to a point. But it often happened that the places did not lend themselves to restoration, so one put the trowel to work, and one built, as for films, complete sets for torture in places where they never existed, or, always in the pious intention of making things appear more probable, one built in Auschwitz and Dachau, for example, some **supplementary** crematoria intended to alleviate the scruples which could have been born in the brains of some mathematicians. It is thus that history will be written: one sees even by this that one can manufacture it. This proves that we have made much progress in the difficult art of propaganda. If the race of historians is not condemned to disappear, it will be advisable to give them all a rigorous archaeological education.[52]

As I am not as intrepid a spirit as the members of the French delegation, I will not conclude from it that there was "will to falsify": but I cannot hide from the reader that **small things** of this kind make me rather circumspect.

The indictment of the French delegation is all the more fragile as it gives us the right to propose complementary testimonies. For he who chooses to prove by the enumeration of testimonies cannot refuse others' help in making this enumeration. And the witnesses that each of us knows afford it more guarantees than the witnesses of the

---

[52] This information has been shown to be somewhat incorrect. One has "put the trowel to work" in order to "restore" the crematory oven of the base camp at Auschwitz (Auschwitz 1), a restoration which historians have judged to be dubious. The other buildings for crematoria, at Birkenau, were blown up before the end of the war and remain in ruins. Later, revisionists have had in effect to metamorphose into archaeologists.

official version. Perhaps the French delegation did not realize it: but its way of proceeding leaves the question open indefinitely. However, the **sincere** witnesses that each of us has been able to meet are far from being as categorical as the official witnesses: or at least they **were** far from being so at the time of their exit from the camps. For there occurred in this regard a very interesting phenomenon. Authentic testimonies, *genuine* ones as the English say, which one could collect in the middle of the year 1945, did not take long to modify themselves. At the beginning, the deportees recounted what they had seen; a little later, they were subject to the influence of the literature of deportation, and they spoke according to the books which they had read and according to the accounts of comrades which gradually replaced their personal impressions; finally, at the last stage, they adopted more or less unconsciously a utilitarian version of their captivity, they became a sounding post[53] for the professionals of political internment, and they replaced in their accounts what they had seen by what it was necessary to say. A small number, on the contrary, underwent a contrary evolution. The exaggerations of the specialized literature disgusted them, they tended to take the opposite course, and it happened sometimes that they, after a lapse of four years, tended to minimize what was inscribed in their memories by scrupules which prevented them from saying anything which was not certain, or by a kind of prudishness about recalling their exceptional lot, or in order not to be confused with the others. It follows that there was a large

---

[53] *sounding post* "(Mus.), a small post in a violin, violoncello, or similar instrument, set under the bridge as a support, for propagating the sounds to the body of the instrument;–called also *sound post*" (*Webster's Revised Unabridged Dictionary*).

variety in the things revealed, and often contradictions: for several things join to produce this, the deterioration which memories undergo depending on family and trade, and relations preserved or broken with former comrades, or the emotional coloring which is given to them by one or another political affiliation. Insofar as the impressions of a deportee could be seized, photographed so to speak, right after his return, and as much as possible before any contamination of his testimony, one comes away with (contrary to what they wanted to prove at Nuremberg) the feeling of a certain diversity.

Let us add finally that testimonies after the trial occurred more or less spontaneously. One learned, in particular, the role of voluntary auxiliaries which certain prisoners accepted in the camps; it was revealed that these prisoners were no strangers to accusations by the victims, that sheltered stations, special functions were allotted under suspect conditions; even some of the witnesses at the trial had already to admit, during a cross-examination, an indirect participation in the mistreatments which are registered in the Bill of Indictment, and it has since been revealed that this participation was often wider, more general than one then believed. The true history of the camps has not been made. We learned that the simple question: "How did you manage to make it out of there?" was a serious question which many survivors cannot answer without embarrassment. What does one have to think, finally, of certain works recently published on the camps? As the block of resistants disintegrates, their spokesmen deviate from the official truth and express themselves more freely about their former associates. One realizes that the solidarity of the deportees was only a figment of propaganda. They themselves now insinuate that things were not as simple as one wanted to make us believe; each party expresses the most serious reservations about the attitude of its adversaries: and finally one recognizes that all these documents on German atrocities must be used with the greatest precaution, for everyone pleads only for himself. Then, from time to time in the general silence, one of these terrible testimonies bursts out, which they delay as much as one can, which they stifle, but which makes one reflect. What truth is there in these *Jours Francs* of Bradley,[54] where one sees the deportees released from a camp in the Rhineland give themselves over for a time to such a drunken binge of torments, massacres, bloody outrages, to such a spasm of sadism and madness, that this orgiastic release, this disemboweling insanity, despite everything that one can recall, makes the scale measuring atrocities lean suddenly unrelentingly to the other side? If all that is true, if it is necessary to take account of this history which continues to be made every day, who can still say that the trial has been adjudicated, who can say that we know the truth about the camps of Germany?

As long as the transcripts of other trials will not have been published—and I think here of the trials of the members of the SD[55] or of the commanders of camps—as

---

[54] *Jours Francs* (*Frank Days*) the title of a book by Jean Bradley, a Frenchman who in 1940 at the age of 17 gave shelter in Paris to an English soldier, was denounced, imprisoned for 3 years and spent another 2 years in various German camps. His book written in 1945 describes the astoundingly barbarous behavior of himself and other prisoners after their release from the camps.

[55] *SD* Sicherheitsdienst, Security Service. This was the German national police force during the National Socialist era.

long as the defense will not have been heard in accordance with all its rights and with all its documents, who will be able to boast that he is able to make a complete and impartial assessment about the concentration camps? When one turns to other testimonies than those which were produced by our propaganda, one suddenly understands the gravity of certain gaps in our information. One realizes that in the version of the facts which was then presented to us there are some accidental elements which we were wrong not to highlight. Most important of all is the effect on camp life of the disorder and the panic that the defeat introduced into the services. The rules which had been laid down for the camps in 1942 or in 1943 were upset, the camps were suddenly over-populated, deluged with prisoners rounded up in the prisons which had been evacuated, deprived of supplies and drugs, abandoned to arbitrariness, disorder, and a famine which became appalling because the supplies ceased to arrive at the moment when the prisoners were flooding in. It is at this time that epidemics appeared, deaths en masse, ferocious fights for the little food which arrived at the camp; it is at this time also that controls disappeared or were weakened and that rage at the defeat, anger at the bombardments, could cause criminal acts which worsened the appalling living conditions created by the disorder. It is under these conditions that the American investigators found the camps: they believed that these conditions were the rule, they did not try to learn how things had been earlier.

And yet rules had existed, the camps had been otherwise. Until the time of the landing,[56] the camps were supervised and inspected, we have been assured of this. They were not to be over-populated, the prisoners were to have four cubic meters of air per person in the barracks. The patients were cared for in the medical ward which could receive (the one described to me) 50 to 60 people; medicines were always provided to the camp in sufficient quantity until the bombardment which destroyed the neighboring city; serious patients were transported to the hospital of this same city. The prisoners had the right to receive parcels: naturally, this priviledge seldom applied to foreign prisoners because their family was unaware of their address, but if their family had been notified of their detention, they could receive parcels like the German prisoners. Tubercular prisoners were kept separate: one could give lethal injections to those who were incurable only with the authorization of the central service of the Gau,[57] and, at the camp in question, this authorization was given only once. At morning roll-call, the prisoners had the right to declare themselves sick and to get themselves examined. It was forbidden to beat the deportees, and several SS were demoted for kickings. The commander of the camp was to submit a monthly report which was transmitted to Berlin and he was subjected to a very strict control. Juridically, the camp was comparable to a prison: that is, the deportees were regarded as accused men whose trials were taking place in military courts functioning in the

---

[56] *landing* sc. at Normandy.

[57] *Gau* a local administrative unit in Germany, somewhat like a French canton.

country where they had been arrested. When the verdicts—given in their absence—were rendered, they were notified if it was a prison sentence. At the end of their prison terms, these prisoners were set free, and there would indeed have been cases where deportees would have been released and returned to their countries, after having signed an agreement not to make any revelation about their camps. On the other hand, when the military court sent a death sentence, the verdict was not revealed. The verdict was regularly recorded in the files of the camp of the Gau SS, and the condemned was executed by an injection of phenol which was presented to him as a vaccination. During the year 1944, there were on the average 600 executions per month for 15,000 prisoners: at that time, deaths by disease, epidemic, and weakening would have amounted to 200 per month. They became much more numerous after the beginning of 1945, for reasons which were stated above and which entailed a complete change in the living conditions in the camp. It was just after this time that a typhus epidemic broke out. This monograph is concerned only with the Belsen camp, close to Bremen, which was a camp of the second category (like Dachau and Sachsenhausen). It is not very probable that one finds an echo of it in the transcript of the Belsen trial, where the defense could not get its witnesses heard because some were defendants whom they refused to believe and the others were illegal immigrants who were in no hurry to be put on display. One will find no more reflection of it in the film devoted to Belsen by the Americans and which was filmed at the end of the year 1945, in which there are some SS sufficiently gaunt to appear, in the eyes of the public, as excellent deportees.

Will one reproach this rectification for being limited to only one isolated case? This objection is valid. I claim to say nothing other than what I have found. But one may presume that there were other cases; there are documents which we should not have ignored, and that fact supports this presumption.

The bulletin copied clandestinely during the occupation by Jewish nationalists is the **only** clandestine voice of the Resistance which gives some precise details on the deportation camps. These precise details were intended for the families. One does not say, naturally, how one got them, but it seems that one can grant a certain credence to them because of their very destination. So here is what one can read in *Shem* July 8, 1944, pages 78 and following: "Information on the camps of deportation. We reproduce below information, which arrived last March, on the camps in Silesia and Poland towards which most of the Jews arrested in France by the French and German authorities were directed... Myslowitz, Hans Well... The living conditions in this camp are catastrophic. The mortality rate is frightening... *Kattovicz-City n • 2*... Food is passable and corresponds to the usual food among the workers in the area. Some craftsmen work in their trade. Some of the latter are authorized to write and receive letters. The women are occupied with housework in the camp and in the kitchen with the preparation of food. In general, the living conditions in this camp are bearable... *Brieg Camp, close to Breslau*... Food is copious but lacks fats. The treatment by the monitoring team is not bad... *Beuthen-Gleiwicz*... The women carry out light ancillary work. They prepare food in the kitchens on wheels... *Myslowicz-Chrzanow-Trzebina Region*... All kinds of craftsmen work here in their trade.

The guard is very severe; it is provided by formations of the regular army. Nevertheless the relations between the supervisors and the interested parties are generally good... *Kattowicz-Birkenau-Wadowicz Region...* The life in these camps is bearable, given their proximity to camps of non-Jewish workers and in some places joint work with them. This work consists of construction of roads, bridges and homes in the cities. These are craftsmen who are well accepted, even preferred here. The morale among the deportees is generally good and they are confident about the future... *Neisse...* Work is very hard and painful, there is insufficient food; the housing of the interested parties is unworthy of a human being... Several cases of suicide occurred... *Oberlangenbielau Camp...* The treatment by the officers in the guard is good, but the monitoring during work is very severe... *Waldenburg in Silesia...* The conditions of existence are very hard... *Theresienstadt.* At one time a small Slovak village with 7000 to 8000 inhabitants, it is today an urban conglomeration with nearly 80,000. This sudden increase is caused by the deportation here of 30,000 to 40,000 Israelites who have repopulated and entirely rebuilt this village." Obviously, on the other hand, it is necessary to remember here the testimonies presented by the Soviet delegation and in particular that which describes the base of extermination at Treblinka, where the Jews were executed en masse right after their arrival in a factitious railroad station which disguised the facilities designed to execute them. One thus sees the difference in treatment between Western Jews and the Jews of Central Europe.

The chronicle of *Shem* 8 continues as follows: "Information could be collected with regard to children, from 2 to 5 years of age, mainly girls. More than 2,000 of these children are distributed among farmers, for the most part among rural families in Eastern Prussia. Some exact and complete addresses of these last will be noted in due course. A persistent rumor (still not controlled) is circulating that in Lauenburg, in Pomerania, as in the frontier march (Grenzmark), there would be some Israelite boys, 5 to 6 years old, in the Hitler Youth. A very great number of infants and babies, less than 2 years of age, from Israelite parents are distributed among various nurseries and numerous day-care centers even in Berlin and in the area around this city. They are always brought there by the DRK (German Red Cross) and the NSVW (German social organization) at the same time as (and as if they were) the children of parents who are disaster victims or who were killed in the air raids, and they are generally received among the orphans as if they were children of this sort. The release of a deportee, officially granted by the central authorities, is generally sabotaged by the subordinates on the spot."

I claim not have provided a basis for a general judgment about the conditions which were imposed on the deportees; nor have I settled the issue of the authenticity of these testimonies, except for their material authenticity: they are to be evaluated, as are all testimonies. I regret only, since it is possible for a private individual to get such information, that no similar deposition appears in the file of the French delegation, and that there was not even an allusion to these facts which are so easy to obtain. This is all the more regrettable since the trial proceeded in the presence of the German public and in front of the members of the German bar, and since, in their country, a principle of jurisprudence, respected by National-Socialism itself, makes it obligatory for the public ministry to mention spontaneously any exculpatory evidence of which it is aware. We see today, with some astonishment, the American military government grant to Ilse Koch[58] a reduction of her sentence, which our newspapers find scandalous. It is perhaps the case that today the American government, better informed about the concentration camps, and in addition a little less sure that it is in its interest to make the Germans pass for monsters, starts to see the exaggerations of its own propaganda.

Would we not do well to consider a correction of our official attitude which the war's proximity and sufferings have made too systematic? We all know that many deportees died without having been exterminated and simply in consequence of the disorder, the crowding and the appalling sanitary conditions which existed in the last months. To say this honestly is not to offend the memory of these people. The French who got information about the last moments of those whom they lost in captivity, if they happen to read these pages, will certainly think that there is nothing incredible in the report which was submitted to me about Belsen. Why then insist on a systematic legend of horror? Of course there were other camps, there was Majdanek, there was Auschwitz, there was Treblinka. But how many French were at Auschwitz, at Treblinka? We will discuss this presently. There was also, and I do not forget it, the

---

[58] *Ilse Koch* the wife of Karl Koch, the commandant of the camp at Buchenwald and later that at Majdanek. She was originally given a life sentence which was commuted to four years; after her release in 1951 she was again arrested, re-tried and given a life sentence. She hung herself in the women's prison at Aichach in 1967. She was a victim of false rumors, such as that she had used lampshades made from human skin.

appalling conditions during the transfer of the deportees. But there still, this is not true of all cases. Certain convoys were awful (*dramatiques*), but many were not. There were medical experiments. This is one of the points on which it would be most important to hear explanations presented by the Germans. Is it correct, as one said at the trial, that these experiments were never required by the Luftwaffe, for the reason that it had already received credit for experiments made on German soldier volunteers? Is it corrrect, as some people have maintained, that the contract offered to the deportees who agreed to undergo these experiments was actually fulfilled and that the deportees who survived were given their freedom? These survivors would have to be shown then: in such a business, this kind of evidence is the only one which is without retort. Lastly, what is the percentage of the French deportees who were the object of medical experiments? This figure has never been provided, it is perhaps difficult to provide, but even a very general approximation would be useful. Would not such clarifications, accomplished without partisanship and not for the purpose of propaganda, be useful to everyone, and to our country in particular? Would not we come off better in all this if our indictment had made known, with honesty and moderation, sufferings which no one disputes and which everyone is ready to respect since they are not accompanied by hatred? Had not that been better than to be exposed to the counter-inquiry of an international commission engaged in filling, as in Belgium after the other war, the gaps in our indictment?

I must repeat: the time has not yet come to write the history of these events and by no means do I regard this small book as a contribution, however humble, to that future work. I bring in no documents; I know no more than anyone else. I simply wrote the reflexions which a reading of the transcript of the Nuremberg Trial inspired in me, somewhat in the manner of those good people of yesteryear who naively thought that their opinion about the Charter[59] or the rights of seniority might interest the public. I needed to write it: that is my only excuse for this indiscretion. But finally in this examination of the third and fourth parts of the Bill of Indictment, this is the kind of work that I previously was taught to a small extent how to do: it is all in all, a criticism of testimony, and I conducted it no differently than I would have conducted an investigation into a historical fact, with the methods which are those that I was taught in criticism and on which all the works of those scholars are founded of whom I was formerly the very modest colleague. That this criticism is so copious is a grave matter. It is a grave matter that the French delegation has mixed everything into its charges, that by biased assertions, by heinous depositions, by bold generalizations, it has compromised what might have been proven with certainty. It is grave matter that it refused to take account of the circumstances, of the historical context, that it isolated facts without saying what had occurred before and what was occurring at the same time. It is a grave matter that it allowed to speak only witnesses about whom one can wonder whether they were interested in the establishment of the truth or in the persistence of propaganda. It is a grave matter that it accepted the procedures of public meetings

---

[59] *Charter* presumably the French Constitutional Charter accepted by Louis XVIII in 1814.

and that it employed a method by its very nature incapable of proving the premeditation of extermination on which the whole indictment was based. It is a grave matter that it claimed human lives while basing its charges on particular facts which point only to the responsibility of the local commanders and which obviously offer no basis for broad generalizations. It is certainly not surprising, but it is hardly honorable for our country that one can read in this indictment sentences like these to **summarize** the attitude of Germany with regard to our prisoners: "Germany multiplied the inhuman treatments which tended to degrade the men whom it held, men who were soldiers and who had handed themselves over, trusting in the sense of military honor of the army to which they had surrendered"; or they even manage to represent as common crimes orders about saboteurs by referring to them as follows: "This paragraph applies to the groups of the British army without uniform or in German uniform." It is not very honorable that our accusation constantly created the impression of being dishonest, and it is not strange that finally the president refused to listen to it at greater length, and that a French magistrate charged to speak in the name of our country saw himself interrupted like an abusive chatterer in one of the greatest trials of history and found no other reply to this bludgeon blow than the pathetic assertion that "he was not expecting this decision."

I repeat: that does not allow one to conclude that the Germans did not commit acts contrary to the laws of war. But that at least makes it possible to say that an inquiry carried out with such bad faith needs to be entirely redone and all its points reconsidered: while waiting for the result of this investigation which must be public, complete and open to rebuttal and cross-examination, it is impossible to take as accurate what was said on this subject by the French delegation, and we have the duty to let it be known publicly that a certain number of men from our country do not accept the current investigation and that they claim the right to suspend their judgment.

Insofar as the German army committed acts contrary to the laws of war, we condemn these acts and the men who are responsible for them, but on the condition that one present them with the circumstances which accompanied them, that one seek out the persons in charge without partisanship, and that such acts be condemned on the part of all belligerents whoever they may be. Concerning this matter we agree with the following two observations by the defense. One is Dr. Babel's declaration, formulated in these terms, which can be accepted, believe me, by any man of good faith in Europe: "This war has brought me so many sufferings and misfortunes that I have no reason to protect or support anyone who was guilty of or an accessory to my personal misfortune and the misfortune which swooped down on all our people. Nor will I try to let such a person escape a just punishment. I endeavor simply to help the court in its search for the truth…" The other is no less moving. It was expressed by this same lawyer, and it is likewise impossible, believe me, for an equitable spirit not to agree with it: "In many cases, acts with which German troops have been charged were caused by the attitude of the civilian population, and acts contrary to the law of nations, when they are committed against Germans, are not judged in the same manner as the misdeeds with which members of the German army have been charged."

In particular, it is not right to claim to shed light on the conduct of the German army in the countries of the Occident without describing the conditions for the occupation which were imposed on it by the Allies' policies. The birth and the development of resistance groups, the attacks ordered by irresponsible organizations, the Jewish propaganda and the actions by Communists, and finally the organization of bands of snipers deeply modified, year by year, the character of the defensive measures which the German army had to take to oppose these initiatives. For their part, the Germans singularly worsened this situation by heavy-handed reprisals or the stupid conscription of workers. But whatever the share of German responsibility in this field, one cannot forget that their adversaries were the first to put themselves in a situation where they had no longer the right (*droit*) to claim the law (*droit*) of nations. The doctrine of the German staff in this matter is not innovative: it was fixed in 1870, it has not varied since then, it is intransigent but healthy. It gives the title of combatants only to troops in uniform, it refuses it to whoever does not make himself known as a combatant by the wearing of a uniform. These doctrines are unattackable. The laws (*lois*) of war have the aim of creating a **closed field** around the combatants. They protect those who look on because they could not be elsewhere, and those who gather the wounded. But from the moment when one of these spectators seizes a rifle and shoots dishonestly from a window at him who fights honestly in the field, he is put outside of the laws (*lois*) of war, and consequently outside of the protection which the laws (*lois*) of war grant to combatants and to non-combatants. The snipers and their auxiliaries, whatever the courage and military discipline with which they fought, are thus only and can be only, from the international point of view, unfair adversaries, cheaters hidden in the area surrounding the arena, who cannot demand for themselves the protection of the laws (*lois*) which reign in the arena, and who are entirely, completely, at the mercy of the winner if they let themselves be captured. Any sniper, any auxiliary or accessory sniper is thus placed outside of the law (*droit*) of nations: in strict application of international law (*loi*), any sniper, any auxiliary or accessory sniper, when he is taken, is a condemned man with a reprieve. This rule is hard: but recent experience proves that its exact observation is the only guarantee for the civilian populations. The men who took on the responsibility of **making the war rotten** (*pourrir la guerre*) by resorting to such methods, took on an appalling responsibility, not only with regard to the men whom they thus exposed to death, but with regard to the civilian populations from whom they withdrew all protection. One cannot say that these men were not informed. The doctrine of the German staff was recalled constantly during this war. It is inadmissible to maintain that it sufficed to mention that we regarded as combat troops a certain number of civilians, whether provided with arm-bands or not, for such conventions are valid only if they are allowed by both sides. When the Germans constitute a **Wehrwolf**[60] to shoot at our occupation troops from hiding places, we explain to them very well that the members of their **Wehrwolf** will be shot if they are taken. Our snipers are only snipers: the fact that they have in their pocket a card for a "progressive" political party does not change anything in their status.

---

[60] *Wehrwolf* or, more correctly, *Werwolf* (German for "werewolf") was a German guerilla movement active for several years after the official end of WW2.

This observation does not erase the wild reprisals exacted by certain German units, but it changes their character. The Allied command intended, with the approach of the landing, to put all the countries of Western Europe in a state of permanent uprising. No German troops, it affirmed, could advance without finding themselves in the middle of traps. Everywhere there were traps and mines under their steps. Each small wood sheltered gunmen, each millstone was a threat, around every bend there was a surprise. Each municipality is praised today for having given supplies to the maquisards,[61] for having hidden them, for having helped them. We are quite imprudent, for such declarations, if we must stand by them, singularly reduce the responsibility of the German commanders. We can accuse them of having illegally extended the concept of "accomplice to a sniper," of having done so most often during times of violent action, and of having done so arbitrarily and without evidence. But that is quite different from the charge made by our Public Ministry. There is no "will to exterminate" in these brutalities from the retreat; there is no "higher order" other than the permanence of an unattackable legal doctrine. There are responsibilities, but they are at the level of the local command. And, moreover, nothing will prevent me from writing that in all these cases these responsibilities are shared by the agitators. It is not only an out of control band of brutes who set fire to the church of Oradour, it is the man who spoke on the London radio and who speaks today on the tombs.

---

[61] *maquisards* members of the *Maquis*, the Resistance.

There are war crimes which are certain and undeniable, and which can be isolated from their circumstances or which the circumstances do not excuse. They are infinitely fewer than the French delegation said they were. When in Baignes, at the time of the Rundstedt offensive, the commander of a group of tanks had managed to encircle a hundred twenty-nine Americans grouped in a field with their arms in the air and then had them machine-gunned; that is an obvious war crime, insofar as the events occurred as they have been described to us. When, following a collective escape, fifty English aviator officers, prisoners at the Sagan camp, are simply selected and shot without a trial, that is also an undeniable and obvious war crime, and a perfectly clear violation of the International Conventions (it is another thing to know if Göring was responsible for this affair). One can say as much about collective reprisals and the burnings of villages, but with the proviso of mentioning expressly that this condemnation encompasses any collective reprisal and any burning of a village, and that the German officers prosecuted for this reason will receive the same punishment as the French officers responsible for similar acts in Indo-China, before and after this war: for, in the end, why should one call the burning of brick houses a crime and the burning of bamboo villages a peccadillo? But it follows from the indictment itself that these undeniable war crimes are few in number and, when one takes care to study some of them, one realizes that they by no means involve the responsibility of the German high command as one wanted to make us believe, but only that of the chiefs of units who did not know how to keep their cool, or who did not know how to maintain discipline, and besides almost always the responsibility of the local Resistance units in the role of agitators. Let us add that some of these acts, at least, were the object of investigations and of sanctions on the part of the German command itself. It is not honest, in any case, to present them pell-mell (to make them appear numerous) with acts much more difficult to judge, assassinations of maquisards (even without trial and even when accompanied by brutalities), executions of saboteurs whose legitimacy is more or less debatable, or lynchings of aviators which the anger of the civilian population explains sufficiently.

It is, moreover, impossible not to step for the moment outside the framework of the trial. If the Germans committed crimes, the men who covered up and caused the atrocities of the liberation are not qualified to serve as their judges. For if it is sad to read the list of the acts declared criminal about which the French delegation complains, it is no less sad to note that for each assassination and rape, for each torture for which one reproaches the German army during the rout, one can cite assassinations, rapes and tortures done by the snipers in what they called their victory. Groups of maquisards were killed without trial, they were tortured before their execution: yes, but militiamen[62] were killed and tortured under the same conditions, in the Vercors, in the Limoges region, in the Périgueux region, in the Toulouse region. Innocent people were hung, their corpses were stabbed with knife-blows at Trébeurden in Brittany, thirty-five Jews were shot without motive at Saint-Amand-Montrond: but it is not only in Trébeurden, it is in twenty, thirty villages from all-over that other innocent

---

[62] *militiamen* (*miliciens*) i.e. members of the *milice* or militia. The *milice* was a paramilitary organization in Vichy France whose purpose was to oppose the Maquis or Resistance.

people, because before the war they had belonged to right-wing parties, were cut down with machine-gun shots in their houses by "patriots," their corpses were mutilated, their eyes blinded, their ears cut off, their genitals torn off, and these are not thirty-five men, but thousands who were assassinated without reason by the "resistants." "Two women, they tell us, were raped at Crest, three women were raped in Saillans... Perraud Lucie, 21 years old, was raped by a German soldier of Russian extraction... rapes, plunderings in the area of Saint-Donat... a civilian was killed in his vineyard... Young men who were walking with girls were killed on a road... Young boys were arrested because they had fled at the sight of Germans... none belonged to the Resistance... Bézillon Andre, 18 years old, whose brother was a maquis, terribly mutilated, nose and tongue cut off ..." Does that not remind you of something? all these sentences from the Public Ministry of de Gaulle's government? How many women were raped in towns and cities terrified by the arrival of the "maquis," how many young people who were walking on roads (I even know of a young girl from near Limoges who was killed on the day of her marriage in her wedding dress), how many people about whom one can say that they belonged neither to the Militia, nor to the L.V.F.,[63] nor to anything at all, how many Bézillon André's, 18 years old, paid for their brother, killed like him, mutilated like him? Be sure, when the reckoning is made, in the race about atrocities, we will lose by only a short head. When one sees the representative of the French

---

[63] *L.V.F. La Légion des volontaires français contre le bolchevisme* (The Legion of French Volunteers against Bolshevism) an organization founded in 1941 by Marcel Déat for the purpose of recruiting Frenchmen to fight on the Eastern front against the Soviets.

delegation recalling the fate of the Maujean family at Tavaux, in Aisne, the mother killed in front of the eyes of the five children, the house burned, the corpse of the mother sprinkled with gasoline, the children locked up in the cellar and rescued just in time by the neighbors, how can one not think of the slaughter at Voiron, where I know not which sympathizers of patriotism believed it necessary to make some two years old and four years old little children atone for their treason? When one reveals to us the death of the commander Madeline, struck with canes of dried ox-sinew, his nails pulled out, obliged to walk barefoot on thumb tacks, burned with cigarettes, it is impossible not to recall at once the almost similar torment of this delegate of Action Française,[64] close to Toulouse, whom they made agonize for four weeks, his members broken, open wounds all over him, in which they had poured gasoline that they lit and acids to make him howl, or the death of the priest of Tautavel, in the area of Perpignan, so martyred that on the morning of his execution, his straw mattress was hardened by his blood, and whose death was so horrible that it awoke for several months superstitions which one had believed abolished for centuries. A band of Mongols crucified a little boy at Presles close to Nice, on the door of a barn; close to Annemasse, "patriots" crucified a man on the ground, after having blinded his eyes. Mr. Dommergues, professor in Besancon, attests that he was struck with canes of dried ox-sinew during his interrogation by the Gestapo, that in a nearby room a tortured woman was howling, that he saw a comrade suspended with a weight on

---

[64] *Action Française* a French monarchist movement founded in 1898 by Maurice Pujo and Henri Vaugeois; it later came under the influence of Charles Maurras. It was dissolved in 1944 but revived in 1947.

each foot, that another had been blinded: but we have the shame to admit that similar things went on for two months in a good number of Gaullist prisons in the Savoy and the South of France, where one could hear each night the cries of tortured prisoners, and where one invited friends and women in order to give them the entertainment of watching it. The very shooting of the hostages of Chateaubriant: who in France knows that there has been a lugubrious counterpart to this? The massacre of the hostages of Fort-Carré close to Antibes was totally similar, with only this difference that the assassination of the hostages was used to mask a settling of accounts.[65] It is too simple to come and explain to us today that these were "Communist crimes." That is not true. They were acts of madmen, and there were madmen in all the camps. All this occurred at the time when the government was under General de Gaulle and he had almost absolute power. Which representative of the **universal conscience** spoke out against it? Which radio?

Alas! one could continue this edifying comparison indefinitely. The acts of madmen carried out by some bands of a broken army, without command, without discipline, during a few weeks in our country, we condemn them indeed and we approve that the individuals responsible for them be sought, but then it is necessary to prosecute on the same basis and in front of the same court the persons responsible for similar crimes committed by certain elements of the Resistance. We too have our war criminals. What will

---

[65] At Châteaubriant twenty-seven Communist hostages were shot in October 1941 in requital for the murder of a German Lieutenant-Colonel. I have been unable to find information about the murders at Fort-Carré.

we reply when the files will all be open? What will we reply when one shows us that wounded Germans were savagely finished off in the streets of our cities, that prisoners were systematically killed after having surrendered their weapons, that unlucky reservists on bicycles, who sought to join a problematic formation, were lynched without reason, disemboweled, hung, decapitated, that inoffensive fifty-year-olds, assigned as guards for a station or a bridge, had to wander for hours while seeking to establish themselves as prisoners of entities who sent them from barracks to barracks and then to teams assigned to massacre them, and that some of them were burned alive in their trucks doused with gasoline? What will we reply when one tells us the true story of what we call the "liberation" of our cities? The Public Ministry can well say at Nuremberg: "at Saint-Donat, in the Vercors, fifty-four women or girls, whose ages ranged from 13 to 50 years, were raped by raging soldiers": but the English and American judges must have some singular reflexions while thinking of the investigation opened by the authorities of the occupation, at the request of the German Episcopate, into the two hundred girls at Stuttgart who were rounded up on Christmas Eve as they left Mass, and were raped in the police stations and barracks where they had been brought. It's a nice thing to explain to us that in the German prisons the prisoners "were savagely beaten," that "children from 18 to 19 years old" were executed, that women were executed, that Jews were kept to dig their trenches, that those condemned to death wore chains on their feet, but which listener is unaware that all that applies word for word to what occurred in our prisons during the Gaullist year? We repudiate, in the name of justice and honesty, this indictment against a gagged country. We refuse the assassins of 1944 the right to speak about humanity. We make a point of saying this to German youth: this masquerade nauseates us and humiliates us, and we refuse to show solidarity with it. France was not that. We will agree to condemn the conduct of the war by Germany only when an international commission carries out an inquiry in all the countries, and ours in particular, on the crimes and the exactions made in the course of the war. The truth is indivisible. Justice too.

As for the concentration camps, honesty consists in our demanding justice and reparations for the innocent French who were deported and tortured, but not for the others. It appears impossible for us to accept, in this field, the confusion about which we spoke above, and which was created intentionally by propaganda. It appears impossible for us not to make, in particular, the distinction which the Germans made between the Jews and the non-Jews. If one refuses this discrimination, one sees only Jews, many Jews, and obviously many deaths. But also one can conclude nothing. – What did the Germans do to you, just to you, in France? – They took away the Jews. – To you, in Belgium? – They took away the Jews. – To you, in Holland? – They took away the Jews. By maintaining this confusion, all that one has the right to say is that the Germans pursued in Holland, in Belgium, and in France, a policy of extermination of the Jews, but then this accusation is no more an accusation by the French people or by the Belgian people or by the Dutch people against Germany; it is an accusation which should be brought by the Jewish people and be supported by Jewish delegates, or by delegates speaking in the name of the Jewish people, and not by any national delegation. However, the various national delegations, and especially the French delegation, carefully maintained this confusion.

It was not said, in Nuremberg, what is the percentage of the Jewish deportees compared to the total of the deportees for each nation. Only one country communicated this figure: Holland, which reported that of 126,000 deportees 110,000 were of the Israelite religion, which gives a proportion of 87%. The French representative in Nuremberg did not believe that he ought to make known these statistics for France; however, in answer to a written question put recently by Mr. Paul Thetten about the number of the victims of the war, the Minister for Ex-Combattants had to put forward a figure: one can read in the *Officiel* of May 26, 1948 that he admitted the existence of 100,000 political deportees and of 120,000 racial deportees, which gives a proportion of 54%. Can this proportion, so different from that which is published by the Dutch government, be accepted? It hardly agrees, in any case, with the documents produced from elsewhere in Nuremberg. One can read, indeed, in the transcript of the trial, that a conference held in Berlin on June 11, 1942 foresaw a transfer of 100,000 Jews residing in France for the year 1942, that the measurements taken for this transfer succeeded only partially, and that the number of the deported Jews amounted to 49,000 on March 6, 1943. Besides , a list of the "deportations of people for political or racial reasons," produced by the French Public Ministry, mentions the following statistics for the convoys: three in 1940, fourteen in 1941, a hundred and seven in 1942, two hundred fifty-seven in 1943, three hundred twenty-six in 1944. Insofar as these statistics are correct and apply well to the convoys of political deportees, it would have to be admitted that in March 1943 one had not reached a quarter of the total number of the deportees. And we know well, indeed, that the rate of the deportations became much faster in 1943 and 1944. Under these conditions, it is not very probable that there were only 120,000 Jews sent into the camps. If the services of the Ministry for Ex-Combattants had not made the declaration which we have just reported, one would have the right to conclude from the documents of Nuremberg that the figure for the Jewish deportees was approximately 200,000 of a total of 220,000 deportees, which would give a proportion similar to that which is published by the Dutch government. There is thus there a contradiction about which it is difficult to decide. For my part, I would be inclined to dispute the figure provided by the Ministry for Ex-Combattants, because this official organization says what it wants, without authorizing anyone to consult its files. While waiting for someone to make known to us the figure which must exist somewhere in the files of the German services, we think that it is essential to take account of the figure acquired for March 1943, and of the acceleration of the deportations after this date.

When one reflects on these figures, it is clear that the trial concerning the concentration camps must be produced under another lighting than that which was arranged up to now: in the thought of the Germans, there was no will to exterminate the French (and this is why one finds no proof of it), but there was a will to exterminate the Jews (concerning this there are numerous pieces of evidence), and there was no deportation of the French, there was a deportation of the Jews; and if certain French were deported at the same time as they, it is because they had accepted or appeared to accept the defense of the Jewish cause.

The whole question is to know if we can admit the German distinction in this debate. However, here is what a Frenchman cannot avoid asking himself. The Jews are originally foreigners, who were initially allowed into our country warily, then in an increasingly large number as some of them obtained influence. In spite of this hospitality which was granted to them, they did not abstain from taking part in the political discussions of our country: and when it was a question of knowing if we would transform the invasion of Czechoslovakia or the war in Poland into an European war, they did not hesitate (it is they who currently affirm this to us) to fight any spirit of conciliation, that is, to involve our country in a disastrous but desirable war, because it was directed against an enemy of their race. We have ceased today being a great nation, we have perhaps even ceased actually being an independent nation, because their wealth and their influence have made their point of view prevail over that of the French who are attached to the conservation of their land and who wanted to maintain peace. We found them then opposed to all reasonable measures which could have preserved our lives and our goods, and at the same time their own lives and their own goods. And, later still, we found them at the head of the persecution and calumny against those of our comrades who had wanted to protect from the rigors of the occupation this country where we have lived longer than they, where our parents have lived, and which the men of our race had made a great country. They say today that they are the true husbands of this land which their parents did not know, and that they understand better than we the wisdom and the mission of this country of which some of them can hardly speak the language: they divided us, they claimed the blood of the best and the purest among us, and they rejoiced and they are rejoicing at our deaths. This war that they wanted, they gave us the right to say that it was their war and not ours. They paid for it the price which one pays for all wars. We have the right not to count their deaths with our deaths.

In spite of the silence imposed on our intellectuals, this effort to pose the Jewish question in concrete terms cannot be eluded. It need not at all be accompanied by anti-Semitism and, for my part, I am not anti-Semitic: I wish on the contrary that the Jewish people find somewhere the fatherland which will enable them to group themselves together. But it seems obvious to me that if I were a refugee in Argentina, I would not concern myself with the internal affairs of Argentina, even if I had obtained the nationality of that country. I would not demand that the Argentinians become the avengers of the persecuted French; I especially would not ask that Argentinians be condemned to death or be imprisoned because they were indifferent to the fate of the French refugees in their land. Why should we feel obliged to avenge and lament in the name of a compatriotism that the law forces us to confess, but which does not touch our hearts? Fraternities are not manufactured. A Jew is for me a man like another, but he is only a man like another; I find it sad that he is massacred and that he is persecuted, but my feeling does not suddenly change, my blood does not suddenly solidify if it is added that he lives in Bordeaux. I do not feel obliged to take up particularly the defense of the Jews, no more than that of the Slavs or that of the Japanese: I would like very much that one cease massacring without reason the Jews, the Slavs and the Japanese, and also the Madagascans, the Indochinese or the Germans of the Sudetenland. That is all. I feel nothing special for the Jews who live France and I do not see why I should. Moreover, the attitude taken by the majority of the Jews with regard to the purification underscored these divergences of sensitivity which an act of naturalization does not make disappear. Many French were ready in 1944, without partisanship, to feel vividly the inhuman treatment which had been inflicted on the Jews; but today other sufferings, other injustices, much more pressing, have drawn our indignation and even our pity. It is the Jews themselves who organized a switching of victims, a switching of injustice. Let them not accuse us of having no heart: we think first of our own, it is they who wanted it so. The purification left in our country bloody scars which will never be forgotten. I would still do, if I had to do it again, what I did during the occupation for the resistants and even for Jews, but I would do it today as Don Juan gives to poor: "for the love of God," and with immense disdain. For it is, indeed, only in the name of this love of God and because they were saved like us by Christ, that we can share today in the sufferings of the Jews. Their reaction to the demands of loyalty, honor and the defense of our land was not the same as ours; this solidarity that we had the right to expect, even in times of ideological war, from co-participants in our nationality, we did not obtain from them; today we can have in regard to them only the impression of a separation, of an incapacity to think of unison, of a failure of assimilation.

It is inevitable then that the extermination of the Jews appears to us now as no more than one of the new procedures of this war which we have to judge as we have to judge the others, the extermination of the Slavs, the bombardments of the large German cities. It is naturally useless to specify that we condemn, like everyone, the systematic extermination of the Jews. But it is not useless to recall that the Germans themselves, as far as we can see by the documents which have reached us, also condemned it, and that the majority of them, even among highest placed, were unaware of it. It clearly results from some of the documents at the trial that **the solution of the Jewish problem**, which had had the approval of the National-Socialist leaders, consisted only of an assembling of the Jews in a territorial zone which one called the **Jewish Reserve**: it was a kind of European ghetto, a Jewish fatherland reconstituted in the East. That is what the instructions known to the ministers and the senior officials envisaged, and it was only that. The defendants of Nuremberg could maintain that they had been unaware during the whole war of the massive executions which took place at Auschwitz, at Treblinka and elsewhere, that they had learned about them for the first time by listening to their accusers, and no document of the trial enables us to affirm that Göring, Ribbentrop, or Keitel lied by saying that; it is very possible, indeed, that the policy of Himmler was a totally personal policy, discreetly carried out, and for which he alone bears the responsibility. The condemnation, in which one asks us to join on this point and in which we do indeed join, thus does not pertain to a people, but to a man to whom the regime was wrong to give exorbitant powers. We do not have the right to conclude from this that the Germans, who were unaware of all that, are monsters. Nor moreover do we have the right to conclude from it that National-Socialism necessarily led to the extermination of the Jews: it proposed only that they no more be allowed to get involved in the political and economic life of the country, and this result could be obtained by reasonable and moderate methods. By setting ourselves up as defenders of the Jewish people, by putting ourselves at the head of a crusade of hatred because of the concentration camps, because of all the concentration camps, by extending this hatred to all, by making it inexpiable and without appeal, are we not victims of a propaganda of which the effects might one day be terribly prejudicial to the French people? What will we reply if one seeks one day to make us carry the weight of this revenge for which we have been volunteers, if one tells us that our complaint, our indictment, should have had as its object only the restricted number of Frenchmen who were deported contrary to the laws of war, if one holds us responsible for this storm of hatred and suffering which we have called down on the German nation which had believed it was treating us gently? Will we reply by speaking about **the great voice of France**? Then let it not keep silent when other injustices and other deaths summon it: if we are by heaven's decree the defenders of everyone, the defenders of the Jews and the Slavs, then we do not have the right to exclude anyone, and we must also be the defenders of the Japanese and the Germans when the corpses are Japanese or German.

I cannot resist then from adding one thing. This mission that we claim for France is singularly compromised, not only by what has happened in our country for four years but also by our silence and on other points by the ease with which we accept all the propaganda. Our indignation undergoes eclipses. Our conscience wakes up when our interest speaks. We denounce the perversity of our adversaries, their coolness before torture and extermination, we pretend to open eyes terrified at the human animal, and we forget at the same time, we forget and we accept the perversity of our own people, we accept the torture and the extermination of our enemies, and we greet as angels of liberation the helmeted beings who are no less monstrous than the monsters of our invention. We are very indignant at the Hitlerian concentration camps, but at the same time we pretend to be unaware of the Soviet concentration camps, which we then discover with horror as soon as our propaganda finds it in our interest. What voice rose to make known to the French public the awful case of the occupation in Germany, who protested against the shameful treatment, indeed "criminal" in the sense of the Geneva Convention, which was inflicted on the German prisoners of war? Our newspapers ensure a broad diffusion for the anti-Soviet propaganda of American origin which is widespread in our country: who sought to check those facts, to at least confront them with documents of Russian origin, finally to speak honestly about Soviet Russia, without being the servant of the Stalinist professionals nor the instrument of American financiers? Where is **the great voice of France**? What truth has it dared to look at directly for four years? We find that war is horrible and we speak about German **atrocities:** but it does not occur to our minds for a moment that it is perhaps an "atrocity" quite as serious to shower whole cities with phosphorus bombs, and we forget the thousands of corpses of women and children huddled up in their cellars, the 80,000 dead at Hamburg in four days, the 60,000 dead at Dresden in forty-eight hours. I do not know what one will think of all that in a half-century. As for me, the American Negro who lowers tranquilly above the houses of a city the lever of his store of bombs appears to me even more inhuman, even more monstrous than the prison warder who, in our imagery, accompanies toward the mortal shower the gloomy columns of Treblinka. And I acknowledge that if I had to make a ranking of both Himmler who undertook the building of the concentration camps and the British air marshal who decided one day in January 1944 to order the tactic of **carpet- bombing** in order to neutralize from then on **the personnel**, I do not think that I would put Himmler in the forefront. But we kissed the Negroes in the streets while calling them our **liberators**, and the air marshal paraded in the middle of our cheers. We are the defenders of civilization, but we support very well the idea that Soviet cities be destroyed in a second by two or three atomic bombs, and we even wish it in the interest of civilization and what is right (*le droit*). And after that we cite with terror the number of the victims of the Nazis.

But there is the perversity, one adds, there is the order, there is this mechanism of horror, this sadism, those people hung while music played, this factory-like decadence (*cet usinage de la déchéance*). Magnificent method which consists in inventing an imagery of horror, then to strike one's chest in the name of all mankind, in honor of the films which we manufacture! Let us first restrain these sensational super-productions worthy of the fertile brains of Hollywood, and we will then see what these beautiful protests are worth which prove above all that we do not have a gift for reflexion. For we have accepted and approved that one set up among us a mechanism for decadence and persecution, we have accepted and approved procedures which involve the same spirit of order, of method, of hypocrisy in the elimination,[66] and which betrays at least as much sadism as that which we denounce in others. Obviously, it is less spectacular than to tear out nails (that, moreover, does not

---

[66] *elimination* the elimination of one's enemies.

prevent the tearing out of nails). But, finally, it is necessary to recognize all the merits, it is necessary to rehabilitate the concept of **moral torture**. The inventors of the ignoble swindle of Article 75,[67] the politicians who protected them, sought to obtain by purely moral means the same results that others sought, according to them, by physical means. They made use of lies, of hypocrisy, of perfidy, to drive men and women to despair, to forfeiture, to material misery and often to physiological misery. Work well done: one does not see blood, and the undertakers take care of the burials, in the hearse for the poor, of course. But tens of thousands of French, those who were among the best of us, the most disinterested, the most honest, the most faithful, are today among the living dead. Driven out of their residences by requisitions, stripped of their savings by confiscations, deprived of their rights as citizens, driven from their jobs, prosecuted by servile judges, overwhelmed by sorrow and bitterness, showered with humiliations and lies, wandering from refusal to refusal, without support, without defenders, they realize today that the city of lies has raised around them invisible walls similar to those of the camps, and that they are condemned, they too, but in silence, to misery and death. Their boys were shot one morning, at dawn. They no longer have anything, they look without understanding at their chests from where one has torn off their cross and their sleeve, the empty sleeve of someone mutilated. They do not wear the pyjamas of the deportees, but they die one evening, like them, inside the invisible prison that injustice built

---

[67] *Article 75* This article of the penal code of 1945 dealt with the crime of intellectual and artistic collaboration with the enemy.

around them. Sometimes, they die modestly of misery, other times they commit suicide with gas, and almost always one explains that the cause is disease, depression, age. All that is not spectacular: there are no whip-blows, but rather summonses, not the drudgery of making soup, but a residential hotel with an alcohol lamp, there is no crematorium, but there are children who die and girls who go away. Yes, Jews, yes, Christian Socialists, Gaullists, Resistants, you can be proud (but these matters will not be forgotten); when one counts the number of these discrete deaths from persecution, one will realize that the figure of 50,000 or 80,000 French dead from deportation is largely balanced by the figure for the French who died from misery and sorrow following the liberation. Since we did not have bombers, we invented a manner of killing within the measure of our means: it is not better than the others, it is only underhanded and cowardly. And I acknowledge that I have infinitely more esteem for the moral courage of Otto Ohlendorf, General of the SS, who recognizes in front of the court that he massacred 90,000 Jews and Ukrainians on the order of his Führer than for the French general who is responsible for as many French deaths but who does not have the fortitude to accept it.

Where did it say that, **the great voice of France?** Where did you see that in the great press and in the radio programs whose job it is to represent us abroad? What "authorized" voice has dared to say, for four years, the whole truth? This secular combat of French thought, which large French newspaper, which great French writer dared to deliver it? We devote ourselves to easier work. We believe ourselves the doctors of the world, but we do not have the courage to place a mirror in front of our eyes. We give moral lessons to the world, and lessons on justice, and lessons on freedom. We are eloquent like a brothel-keeper giving sermons. Our great idea is that morals and justice are always on our side. Then, we have the right, we and our friends, to a certain liberty of action. It is for a good cause. What we do, what our allies do, these are never atrocities. But as soon as a regime is our adversary, atrocities sprout up around it like nettles in a garden.

I will believe in the judicial existence of **war crimes** when I see General Eisenhower and Marshal Rossokovsky take seats at the Nuremberg Court on the bench for the accused. And beside them, some lesser notables, like our General de Gaulle, who was responsible much more directly than Keitel and Jodl for a good number of atrocities. While waiting, I do not care to make the mill of curses turn in the direction of the various enemies of the City and of Wall Street or to change anathemas as women change hats. I claim the right not to believe in the accounts of war correspondents. And I claim the right to reflect before becoming indignant. The oil map (*carte du pétrole*)[68] seems to me a little too complicated for my philosophy.

* * * * *

One could believe here that the principles laid down in this third part are unattackable and lucid, and that there is

---

[68] *carte du pétrole* might also mean a "(rationing) card for gasoline." It seems to be so taken in the Italian translation available at the AAARGH website where it is rendered as *tessera della benzina*. The comment, in which this phrase is found, remains in any case (to this reader) inscrutable. The German translation omits it.

nothing simpler than to condemn acts contrary to the laws of war. That is what would have occurred indeed if the court had been satisfied to note that the German army had committed acts expressly prohibited by the Hague Conventions. We do not have anything to say when it restricts itself to doing that, to the conduct of the war on the sea, for example, or to irregular executions of prisoners of war or to abusive requisitions: but, apart from this final chapter which is moreover an extremely complex question, these accusations are not numerous and, more importantly, they are not the essence of the trial. This last part of the Bill of Indictment raises all kinds of difficulties, and some of them are very grave, precisely because the court wanted to innovate.

It recognizes this innovation. The retroactive character of the international law improvised by the court is so obvious that it was not denied by the chiefs of the English and American delegations. They excuse themselves for it only by saying that world-wide public opinion would not understand their leaving unpunished certain cold-blooded atrocities. What does this assertion mean when world-wide public opinion has been intentionally overheated, and as long as a complete and honest investigation has not been opened against all the belligerents. In the absence of these guarantees, the meaning of the retroactivity of the international law is in the end as follows: Allied diplomats meet in London after the signing of the capitulation, and declare that such and such acts for which they reproach their enemies will be regarded as criminal and will be punished by death; they make a list of them, a list which they call the Statute of August 8, 1945, and they hire judges to make up a Bill of Indictment of which every paragraph ends with this exorbitant sentence: "and these acts committed in 1943 or 1944 are illegal and criminal, since contrary to Article 6 or Article 8 of our statute." Children, at least, say *pouce*[69] when they want to change the rules of the game. But our international lawyers did not shy away from this inconsistency: they do not even appear to have seen its consequences.

For, what is striking is not only the unjust character of this retroactivity rejected by all legislators, it is its danger for the future. It is quite obvious that after any international war the winner will believe himself from now on authorized to do the same. He will claim for himself also the indignation of world-wide public opinion. He will have no trouble getting people to admit that the persons in charge of the atomic bombardments must be prosecuted. He will be able to get them to admit as well that the persons in charge of all the bombardments of civilian populations must be prosecuted on the same basis. And he will punish pell-mell the aviators, the generals, the ministers, the manufacturers, by following this precedent. He will even be able to go further. It is enough to be strongest. One can support with very good arguments that any blockade operation is essentially inhuman and declare it contrary to the laws of war. The stronger can declare all that he wants: his photographers will publish pictures of corpses, his journalists will make reports and world-wide public opinion will quiver while listening to its radio. And his enemies will be hung, down to the rank of colonel, without exception, or further if

---

[69] *pouce* "thumb" or "inch." It means : "stop it".

it is his good pleasure. "I want to win the next war," Marshal Montgomery said in a recent interview, "for I do not care to be hung." This British military man has well understood the firmness of the new law.

The French delegation, the embodiment of logic and firmness, was sorry to hear this word **retroactive**. It wanted to show that one must not have all these scruples, and that Mr. Göring was juridically only a highwayman. And here is the firm step which it took to prove it: it is interesting for us since it lays down a principle broader than the previous one. The Germans, **having been the aggressors**, the war which they make is **illegal**, and they put themselves thereby outside of international law. "What does that mean, if not that all crimes which will be committed following this aggression for the pursuit of the fight thus started will cease having the judicial character of acts of war?" From then on, all becomes very simple: "Acts committed for the pursuit of a war are attacks on people and on goods which are prohibited and sanctioned in all legislations. The state of war could make them licit only if the war itself were licit. But subsequent to the Briand-Kellog Pact there are no more such wars; hence these acts become purely and simply crimes against common law." So there it is. It is no more difficult than that and it was enough just to think so: **we**, all that we do is **licit**, those are **acts of war**, which are covered by a "special rule of the international law ... which removes from so-called acts of war any penal qualification," **they**, all that they do "for the pursuit of the fight thus started" (a very vast expression) is **illicit** and thereby becomes even a crime against common law. On one side, order, gravity, conscience: the armies of the right (*droit*) bombard Dresden with a feeling of infinite sorrow, and when our Senegalese rape the girls of Stuttgart, it is an act of war which eludes any penal qualification; on the other side, the common law[70] in uniform and helmut: a troop of brigands wearing various disguises moves into a cave called Kommandantur, and all that they do is called plundering, sequestration, assassinations. It is not I who say this, it is again the French delegation. "The putting to death of the prisoners of war, of the hostages and of the inhabitants of the occupied territories, falls, in French law, under the scope of Articles 295 and following of the Penal Code, which delineate murder and assassination. The mistreatments to which the Bill of Indictment refers fall into the category of wounds and voluntary blows which are defined by Articles 309 and following. The deportation is analyzed, independently of the murders by which it was accompanied, as an arbitrary sequestration, as described in Articles 341 and 344. The plundering of public and private property and the imposition of collective fines are sanctioned by Articles 221 and following of our Code of Military Justice. Article 434 of the Penal Code punishes voluntary destruction, and the deportation of civilian workers is assimilated to forced enrollment, as envisaged by Article 92." And there it is; that's how the naughty word retroactivity was erased from our papers. All that thanks to this good little Briand-Kellog Pact, a dusty crossbow taken down off its hook in the attic; however old, it has served to shoot off these beautiful fireworks.

---

[70] *common law* By "common law" Bardèche here surely means "common law criminals," but curiously does not say that: "de l'autre côté, le droit commun en uniforme et casqué."

The ignoble and monstrous character of this judicial swindle deserves to be underlined. For that purpose it should be known that the acts thus defined by our delegation are, in addition, expressly recognized as rights by The Hague Conventions. Armies in war have the right to take hostages, and we have set no restrictions on their doing this; they have jurisdiction over prisoners of war under certain formal conditions; they have the right to ensure order in areas behind the lines and to make arrests; they have the right to condemn and execute agents of the enemy in occupied territory and, in particular, snipers. They have the right to note "normal" expenses of occupation and to proceed to requisitions while following certain rules. Such is the right (*droit*) of war, the right (*droit*) of nations, written and agreed upon, and it is this right (*droit*) of war, this right (*droit*) of nations, that our delegation denies to our enemies. International law (*loi*) exists: but it does not exist for them. We, the army of the Right (*Droit*), we have a share in all that: not they. And this is all the more beautiful since, while the Germans were here, **while they were the strongest**, we made demands from them for ourselves on the basis of international law (*droit*). When they were the strongest, they were soldiers and they **were obliged** to apply the law (*droit*) of nations, and we accepted in many circumstances to profit from it. Now that they are vanquished, they are no longer soldiers, they no longer have the right (*droit*) to claim the law (*droit*) of nations in their turn, they have become common law (*droit*) criminals. It is difficult to be more ignoble and low. But, since our "resistants" are conscienceless, they are still astonished when we tell them that the French policy since 1944 is for us only a mark of baseness, a subject of shame, and an image of dishonor.

Besides one will recognize a certain unity in the "thought" of Mr. de Menthon.[71] Its system consists in denying reality. To us other French he says: there was no armistice, there was no French government in Vichy, the war continued, the French government sat in London, and any Frenchman of the metropolitan territory who addressed a word to the enemy can be charged with intelligence with the enemy, he was not performing a political act, he committed a common law crime envisaged by Articles 75 and following of the Penal Code. To the Germans, he explains in the same way: there was no war, there was no German army, but just a gathering of brigands associated for the perpetration of common law crimes, and any German who signed an order was a criminal shouting something to his accomplices, he was not performing an act of war more or less in conformity with the International Conventions, he committed a common law crime or he made himself an accessory to common law crimes envisaged by Articles such and such of the Penal Code.

It is admirable to live with so much ease in an upside-down universe. Intellectual dishonesty cannot go further. A fundamental lie, a madman's howl reflected by a thousand echoes is the prelude of this legislator. One says to him: "and yet she's turning,"[72] but he does not hear, he goes as a blind man transported by his bad faith and his hatred, he staggers in the middle of enormities. And he invites us to

---

[71] *Mr. de Menthon* See note 15 above.

[72] It is unlcear who or what "she" is.

contemplate his monstrous puppets, his allegories which go with their heads down, with the Truth playing the clown in his circus and Justice walking on the ceiling like flies.

One perceives easily that this principle is much more fertile than the previous one. From now on, any international war becomes **automatically** a war of the Right (*Droit*). The winner will have no trouble making it recognized that the vanquished is always the aggressor. We have good examples of this. Nothing is more confused than the beginning of the hostilities in Poland. We have **forgotten** the Polish provocations, sufficiently copious that the German government could assemble them into a *White Book*.[73] And nothing is more confused than the business about Berlin. The Soviet government deduces with logic and correctness the consequences of the non-sensical agreement which has been made with it. That does not mean that if the war breaks out, one will not designate it as the aggressor. Let us see things as they are. The Briand-Kellog Pact is, actually, a magic wand in the hands of the winner. And any successor of Mr. de Menthon will have from now on the right to repeat Mr. de Menthon's reasoning, and to explain to the vanquished that they were not soldiers as they believed, but a band of criminals gathered (according to the case) for an attack on liberty or an operation of capitalist brigandage. Justice has from now on disappeared from our world. International law (*droit*) is not only an equivocal law (*droit*),

---

[73] *White Book* (*Livre Blanc*) A "White Book" is a text drawn up by a government containing proposals put forth by a previous administration. A "Green Book" is a text drawn up by a government containing its own proposals. For a fuller discussion (in French), cf. http://www.europeplusnet.info/article529.html.

it is finally, such as it is applied today, the negation and destruction of all law (*droit*).

This destruction of law (*droit*) has immense consequences. The law (*droit*) which protects is the written law (*droit*). And it is not non-existent in international law (*droit*) since there have been the Hague Conventions. The law (*droit*) is the edict. The edict is a sure thing: one sees written on the wall that which is allowed and that which is forbidden. But today one cannot say, during a war, nor even perhaps in full peace, what he might or might not be reproached for. The **international conscience** will judge. And what will one make it say, the **international conscience**? How did our lawyers not see that this new basis for international law (*droit*) was nothing other than this *Volksempfinden*[74] for which they reproached National-Socialism so much? Thus this elastic world, that we described at the beginning of this book, is much more still than we could imagine. All is common law (*droit*) if one so wants. There are no more armies, there will never again be armies. In the eyes of the winner, there is only a band of criminals perpetrating crimes against him: he is forbidden to address a word to these criminals, forbidden to regard them as men, forbidden to think that they perhaps sometimes speak the truth. He is especially forbidden to make deals with them: one is in a permanent state of war with crime. But on which side is the crime? The frontline is likely to become in these matters the highest authority: the American

---

[74] *Volksempfinden* folk-feeling, i.e., feelings or sensitivities shared by members of a particular ethnic group.

uniform is the livery of crime if Moscow wins, and Communism is the last degree of barbarity if Magnitogorsk[75] capitulates. This new law (*droit*) is not so new as it may seem. Between Mahometans and Christians, one reached decisions in much this way, and, to escape the massacre, there remained as nowadays the resource of conversion. But it is rather funny to call that progress.

This spirit of our new legislation is worsened still more by the modern conception of responsibility. If we had been wise, it was not very difficult to disentangle the responsibilities. It is clear, it is admitted by all the courts of the world, that when a subordinate carries out an order, he is protected by this order itself. His personal liability starts only from the moment when he himself adds some aggravating measure. If a police officer receives the order to question a suspect, he cannot be worried about having questioned and arrested him, but if he tears his eye out, it is just that one prosecute him for having torn out an eye of a prisoner. This reasonable and traditional manner of interpreting the laws permitted us to seek the authors of mistreatments and tortures, and we here protest by no means against the particular trials in which torturers were prosecuted, when these trials were regular and when the judgment was given in accordance with the articles of the code which punish mistreatments and torture. It was even possible, under these conditions, to seek the officers who were directly responsible for hasty or exaggerated reprisals and to accuse them of

---

[75] *Magnitogorsk* a city in southwest Siberia, which has a large iron mine and was a center for steel production during World War II.

having exceeded their orders or of having interpreted general instructions with such a brutality that that was equivalent to exceeding the orders given. These individual trials were all the more legitimate since one found in the majority of the cases infringements to the Hague Conventions, and since, consequently, one innovated in no regard and one was satisfied to prosecute murderous abuses of power. This reasonable manner of rendering justice would have rallied the consciences of everyone. It did not put an abyss between the German people and us. The winner only said: "There are laws of war and you knew them, we punish equally in your ranks and ours those who did not observe them, and now we ask you to forget your sufferings as we try to forget ours, let us rebuild our cities and live in peace." Thus would have spoken just men.

But that did not suit us. We were determined to punish not merely isolated criminal acts: it had to be affirmed that the **whole** German policy was criminal, that this whole war was a long string of crimes, and that, consequently, every German was a criminal, since he had collaborated, even without initiative, even like a simple instrument, with this criminal policy. It was necessary to be able to maintain that in the most strongly disciplined country which exists and which was under the most absolute regime, and although this regime was for ten years the legal regime, recognized by the whole world, nevertheless the laws, the ordinances, the payments, the orders emanating from this government **had no value**, and protected the executants not at all. Then we refused to recognize anything for what it is, we trampled under our feet the most obvious and elementary evidence. What we have come to maintain surpasses imagination. We have forgotten, we have refused to see that the *Führer-Prinzip*, the basis for the German legal regime, made of each private individual a soldier, of each executant a man who did not have the right to discuss the orders, whatever his rank. What ought someone to have done who had the misfortune of being a German general? They were absolutely forbidden to resign during the war. What then? Our "justice" allows them to choose between the stake[76] for refusal to obey and the gallows of Nuremberg for having fulfilled the orders. They ought to have protested? But they did protest. The file of the Allies in Nuremberg consisted essentially of reports and protests which the executants of the highest ranks addressed to the District General of the Führer to describe the excesses to which the conduct of the war gave occasion and to demand that one reconsider the too severe orders which had been transmitted to them. They were regularly told in response that the Führer or his delegate, Reichsführer-SS Heinrich Himmler, maintained these instructions and that they took full responsibility for them.

There was a responsible person in Germany, and there was only one, that was Adolf Hitler. One did not discuss an order of Adolf Hitler. All the greatest said it, and Göring himself said: we were not always in agreement even on essential points, but once the order was given, the duty was to obey. This absolute discipline, inscribed in the oath of fidelity, was presented to the Germans as the basis of their regime, and also as a guarantee with regard to their conscience. We know this extremely well and our "judges"

---

[76] *stake* i.e., death before a firing squad.

know it extremely well. But, then, here is what they invented. Contrary to the legislation of the German State, and contrary also to all national legislations, they did not fear to declare first of all that no one could regard himself as covered by higher orders. That was their statute, written in August 1945, which firmly established this new principle: "The statute establishes that he who has committed criminal acts cannot find excuses in higher orders." Sir Hartley Shawcross, the British prosecutor, drew the following consequence from this declaration: "Political honesty, military obedience are excellent things, but they do not require or justify the commission of notoriously bad acts. There comes a moment when a man must refuse to obey his chief if he wants to obey his conscience. Even the simple private serving in the ranks is not obliged to obey illegal acts." This assertion, if serious since it makes compulsory conscientious objection, is not however enough for the Court, which found a means to come back to this point in the Judgment itself. "He who has violated the laws of war, concludes the Court, cannot, in order to justify himself, plead the mandate which he received from the State, once the State, by giving this mandate, has exceeded the powers which international law recognizes in it. A fundamental idea of the statute is that the international obligations which are imposed on individuals have precedence over their duty of obedience towards the State of which they are citizens."

    One could not wish for more precise assertions, and this political philosophy has, at least, the merit of being clear. It sets up conscientious objection as a duty. It imposes the refusal to obey. Its hatred of military States is such that it destroys the entire State. What was the honor and the drama of the soldier are denied by it in one single sentence. The grandeur of the discipline is crossed out with the stroke of a pen. The honor of the men, which is the honor of a faithful servant, honor such as it has been written in our consciences since the first oath sworn to a sovereign, this honor exists no more, it is not inscribed in the civic instruction manual. Only our expert judges did not see that, by destroying the **monarchical** form of fidelity, they destroyed all the fatherlands: for there is no regime which does not rely on the contract of service, there is no sovereignty other than the monarchical, and the republics themselves have invented the expression, a "sovereign people."

From now on, this conscience which is clear about its duty is no more, the order of the sovereign is deposed from its absolute power. The indisputable, the certain is abolished everywhere. The edict placed on the wall no longer has any authority, obedience to the magistrate is a matter of circumstance. It is no more permitted to anyone to say: the law is the law, the king is the king. All that was clear, all that enabled us to die tranquil is undercut by these absurd sentences. The State no more has a form. The city no more has walls. A new sovereign, without a capital and without a face, reigns in their place from now on. Its tabernacle is a radio. It is there that one hears each evening the voice to which we owe obedience, that of the Super-State which has primacy over the fatherland. Because the sentence written by the judges in their Judgment is clear, it leaves no place for ambiguity: if the **conscience of humanity** has condemned a nation, the citizens of that nation are released from their bond of obedience, and not only are they released from it, but they **must** act against their own country: "the international obligations which are imposed on individuals have precedence over their duty of obedience towards the State of which they are citizens."

Thus, at this point of our analysis, one discovers that everything holds and fits together well. We are no more the soldiers of a fatherland, we are the soldiers of the moral law. We are no more the citizens of a nation, we are consciences in the service of humanity. All then makes sense. It is not a question of knowing whether Marshal Pétain is the legal chief of the government of France: France does not exist; legality does not exist; it is a question of knowing whether General de Gaulle incarnates international morals more exactly than Marshal Pétain: between the **democracy**, incarnated by a committee improvised in London, and **France,** represented by a government which does not convene the general councils, there can be no hesitation: one must prefer the democracy, because morals are necessarily on the side of the democracy, while France . . . that does not represent anything with regard to morals. There we are: we are thus in the presence of the complete intellectual landscape of the brain of Mr. de Menthon. From now on, it is **democracy** which is the fatherland, and the fatherland is nothing any more if it is not democratic. To prefer the fatherland to democracy, that is treason. When democracy is threatened, patriotism is **always** on the side of democracy. If the fatherland is in the opposite camp, that makes no difference: in that case, **resistance** is the supreme law, **treason** is obligatory and fidelity is treason, it is the sniper who is the true soldier.

There again, the new situation defined by the Court should not surprise us so much. For it has a precedent which well establishes its purpose: it is quite simply an excommunication. And the results that one expects from it, the results that one demands from it, are indeed the results that the Church expected and demanded from a bull of excommunication. The State, thus condemned, must be emptied immediately of its energy and substance, it must inspire from one day to the next horror and fear, one must refuse it bread and salt, that is, taxes, service, obedience; its generals must revolt. The French delegation even informs us that this excommunication has the power to change the name and the character (*qualité*) of anything. That which is stubborn is metamorphosed as by the wand of a fairy. The excommunicated army is no more an army, it becomes a criminal conspiracy; acts of war are no more acts of war, they become crimes of common law. The legal curse transforms the country into a desert and at the same time it transforms all its inhabitants into subjects of the empire of evil; it removes from them the prerogatives of a human being. If they do not join the party of the angel, if they do not call upon their cities exterminating lightning, they are enveloped in the curse and the condemnation of their country. If they do not call their fatherland Sodom, and if they do not curse it, there is no mercy for them. The U.N. fulminates and the fatherland dissolves. Temporal power is no more.

It is indeed to this dissolution of temporal power that we are brought little by little by the tendencies which we were describing in the course of our analysis of the first and the second sections of the Bill of Indictment, and of which we find here the full expression. We had concluded previously that it was nationalisms and with them the modes of expression or of defense of nationalisms which were attacked by the spirit of Nuremberg. The new law led to a dispossession. We see now that it is not only nationalisms which are put under indictment, but the fatherlands themselves. Internal laws are dethroned by the advent of a higher law; sovereign States are deposed if they do not agree to be the servants of the Super-State and its religion. But it is not only that. The Messianic spirit is unmasked in the end: it says clearly its new Gospel. All cities[77] (*cités*) are suspect. They are in reality only the agents of the power. Their temporal power is no more than a power of administration. The fatherlands are now only managers of an immense anonymous company. One leaves them a certain power of regulation: their domain is so circumscribed and defined, but in essence they are dispossessed. The spiritual power, the power to reassure consciences, to make legitimate what is in conformity with the law, does not belong to them any more. As managers of the temporal, they must bow and be silent, as soon as it is a matter of State decisions. And not only one invites them to be silent, but one invites the citizens to mistrust their cities (*cités*). The fatherlands can give birth only to heresies. They are all suspected of being under an original curse. They are declared unable to formulate dogma and are suspect even when they interpret it. One withdraws from them any power over consciences. The spiritual is confiscated for the benefit of a higher international authority. It is that which says what is just, it is that which is the conscience of the world. The fatherlands are deposed. They are deposed for the benefit of a spiritual empire of the world which "has precedence," as they say, over all the fatherlands. They reinvented Rome. There is from now on, there is officially since the judgment of Nuremberg, a

---

[77] *cities* See note 7 above.

religion of humanity, and there is also a **catholicism** of humanity. We owe submission to the very holy church of humanity, which has bombers for missionaries. The judgment of Nuremberg is the bull *Unigenitus*.[78] From now on, the conclave pronounces and the sceptres fall. We enter the history of the Holy Empire.

This notion of a universal State having control over consciences is thus only the crowning of the principles which we had seen laid down before. Without this finishing touch, they look incomplete: but with it, all is cleared up, this dome gives its true form to the building. We were told, first, that we should not join together to give strength and grandeur to our cities, and that these unions could at any moment be called criminal conspiracies; and, secondly, that we must get used to delegating part of our sovereignty, the essential part, as stated in the terms of the Constitutional Charter of the Super-State, which was **granted** to the world without anyone asking our opinion. These provisions bind us twice over, they bind us in our cities and in our relationships with foreigners, in what is called in the newspapers domestic policy and foreign policy. The universal conscience, judging from its court on high, has forbidden us defense and has forbidden us isolation. But that was not enough. It is necessary that it take its conscience business to the very end: it is necessary that it, like the eye of Cain, be installed in the

---

[78] *Unigenitus* ("only begotten") the first word of an anti-Jansenist papal bull of Pope Clement XI in 1713.

tomb.[79] It represents the gaze of God. It prohibits and makes one tremble. It is suspended like a sword. The magistrate returns home with his head bowed to his shoulders, the police officer coughs very loudly before stopping at the den, and the general feels the cord around his neck. For the conscience does not write anything, it indicates only a line to be followed, **the line**. It is not coercion, it does not have gendarmes, there is only one poison in the State, a simple infiltration which corrupts all. You are not even threatened, it is your own voice which threatens you, for the universal conscience is everyone, and it is even you. Are you sure that you have acted in accordance with morality, with this universal morality for which we all carry the instinct in us and which will wake up on the day of judgment and which will **spontaneously** demand punishments? Are you sure of having been in **the line**? Which line? says the general: they all say the same words, but these words do not mean the same thing. That makes no difference, do not worry about that: do you have a conscience, yes or no? Everyone, even a general, has a conscience. Then you lead according to the inalienable laws of the conscience, and according to them alone, or otherwise you will be hung. Remember that there are no rules for infantry, that there are no rules for service in a campaign, that there are no higher orders, that nothing that is written means anything, that all our laws are minor laws covered (*couvertes*) in any case by the great voice of the universal conscience, which is most often transmitted by radio, that the unity of the State and the existence of the

---

[79] In Victor Hugo's poem *La Conscience*, after Cain's murder of Abel the eye of God follows Cain everywhere, even into a tomb which he has built for himself to live in, in an effort to escape it.

State can at any moment be declared dissolved by a simple bull, and that nothing exists, absolutely nothing, except the voice which comes from on high.

Here is the world which has been made for us, quite simply because it was necessary that the Germans be monsters and that those be right who had crushed their cities. To justify the destruction, one invents continual destruction. To justify the radio, one invents the radio for perpetuity. To justify the Allies, one swears that all wars must be conducted from now on like the preceding one. Under the pretext of attacking an authoritative regime, one has destroyed authority everywhere, and under the pretext of condemning Germany, one has shackled everyone. We have let ourselves act in the name of virtue and a better world, without seeing that this Super-State which prohibits by principle certain forms of State, which dictates the contracts and which supervises the policies, is nothing other than an anonymous suzerain who regulates the condition of his vassals. International morality is only the instrument of a reign. It is impotent to protect individuals, but it is very useful for dominating States.

It is hardly necessary to underline here how useful this beautiful preliminary work can ultimately be for the universal reign of Marxism, whose Gorgon face one pretends to perceive today. For in the end what else does Marxism maintain—but with another meaning for the words? For Marxists, indeed the national law in each country is "trumped" (*primé*) by the duty which is binding on individuals to take part in the liberating struggle of the proletariat. For them, indeed, there is always above their obligations as citizens a universal conscience which is nothing other than class consciousness. This Marxist conscience upbraids in the same terms, and is likewise vague; with it too it is a matter of being **in line**. The theorists of the universal conscience did not see very well that this weapon to which they give so much care is similar to that javelin of the Australians which can always return to strike the thrower. All that they do can be turned against them. All that they affirm can serve their enemy. And we should not be astonished today if the Communist Party informs us that "the French people" will not accept the war against Russia: that is an application of the principles of Nuremberg. For in the end, Nuremberg destroys fatherlands: who destroys them better than Communism? Nuremberg founds an international authority: is not Moscow one?

Nuremberg creates a Church: there exists another which is the Third International.[80]

Nuremberg decrees the reign of the universal conscience: it will be enough for Bolshevism to disguise itself with this skin so as to appear as good as they.[81] Our theorists transformed all wars to come into civil wars, and in these civil wars they have prepared all that will serve their adversary. Mars is no more the god of war, but *Janus*

---

[80] *Third International* the Third International Communist Congress, held in Moscow in March 1919.

[81] "They" here refers seemingly to representatives of the universal conscience, like the "theorists" in the next sentence.

bifrons,[82] Janus with the two ears who does not know to which radio to dedicate himself. They disarmed us against foreigners. But which?

Another result obtained is that of the real deposition of the human person, which is inseparable from the deposition of the fatherlands. This second result is initially more surprising than the first, because the Nuremberg Court took as its theme the defense of the human person. But this unfortunately is nonetheless certain.

Hear us on one point. It is not a question of denying that the precise regulations and prohibitions concerning the law of nations and the conduct of war, which one finds in the Judgment of Nuremberg and which from now on constitute jurisprudence in this matter, cannot render great services for the protection of people. The Hague Conventions were thus supplemented by many texts which modern war had made necessary. It had been however in the interest of everyone that this new code of war be instituted under different circumstances, following an honest and complete co-operation among all nations, and especially that it not seem tied to a political conception of the world. It would have been better to stick to practical and clear texts, rather than to formulate an ambitious philosophy of the law of nations which risks being interpreted in the most surprising way. It would have been more useful also to propose a complete examination of the procedures of modern war rather than to leave in our coding gaps as

---

[82] *Janus bifrons* "two-faced Janus," the Roman god of gates, doors, beginnings and endings.

serious as those concerning blockades and bombardments of civilian populations, simply because these subjects for thought were inopportune.

But that is not the issue here. We take the expression **defense of the human person** in the most general sense that it was given during the recent discussions. It is rights, it is the freedom of man which is the concern of those who employ these words. It is this sense which we give them too.

We will not hold against the representatives of the universal conscience their impotence to ensure respect for human dignity, even in the territories controlled by it.

That would be too easy a game. There are obviously all kinds of people who, at present, cannot claim to pass for **human persons**: for example, the Indochinese whom we massacre in Indo-China, the Madagascans whom we imprison in Madagascar, the Baltic peoples, the Sudetens, the Germans of the Volga who make great tourists in the centers of D.P.,[83] the little Nazis, the average Nazis and other monsters whom one is obliged to lock up in Dachau and Mauthausen, the Poles and the Czechs who do not like the Soviet government, the Negroes of Louisiana and the Carolinas, the French who shouted: "Long live the Marshal," the Arabs who shouted: "Long live the Sultan," the Greeks who shouted: "Long live Greece," and the Ukrainians whom one sends to Siberia because they have the misfortune of being surviving Ukrainians… I allow that all that does not

---

[83] *D.P.* Displaced Persons.

prove anything, though I find this list a little long. I am only distressed by the fact that, in adding them all up, one finds in the end more corpses, tortures and deportations on the record of the professional defenders of the human person than on that of those whom they call torturers and murderers.

But let us then accept that that does not prove anything. I do not understand very well how that does not prove anything, but let us believe it, since very serious minds tell us it. What is important, moreover, is not to show that the defense of the human person accomodates at present murders, tortures and deportations, but rather to show that in reality it can lead in the end only to the deposition of the human person.

The inevitability of this, however, has been spelled out in quite clear terms, and we have all been able to read it more than once. The defense of the human person is not a new religion. This god has already been proposed to us for adoration. His arrival always takes place in the middle of the same festivals: the guillotine is his high priest and the throats of a great number of oppressors are cut in honor of the god. Thereafter, the ceremony regularly terminates with a fine-looking authoritative regime, resplendent with helmets, boots, shoulder pads, and abundantly decorated slavedrivers. This inherent contradiction has very often been mentioned; and even before the war, the most serious observers had already begun to agree to recognize (something which one hardly mentions any more) that the word "freedom" is most habitually used by scoundrels. Thus history leads us to a first contradiction which is regularly inscribed in the facts: the defense of the human person can terminate only in oppression in the name of freedom, or in hypocritical regimes which save freedom only by closing their eyes to the degradation of persons. Geography is no more consoling. The respect for human dignity consists in recognizing an equal human essence in all (*une égale spécificité humaine*) and consequently equal rights for the Negro of Douala and the Archbishop of Paris. One cavels about equal rights: it will certainly be necessary one day to recognize them or our motto[84] will no more make sense. From this day forward, the free expression of the equal rights of two billion human beings is distributed as follows: 600 million whites, and the rest in Negroes, Asians or Semites. By what reasoning will you make the Negroes, Asians or Semites admit that their equal rights cannot be expressed in equal representation, and that, when it concerns serious matters, the opinion of a white is worth that of ten blacks? There is only one argument which makes perceptible a truth so little evident; it is the presence of Her Majesty's fleet, to which one has recourse indeed each time the discussion threatens to go astray toward generalities. Thus, the defense of the human person still terminates in the same contradiction: it is established with canon shots, or it consists in hearing submissively whatever orders it will please the *colored gentlemen* to give us.

Here, however, is that for which we are making so much noise: for a freedom that we cannot make reign, and for an equality which we refuse to actualize. *Verba et voces.*[85]

---

[84] *motto* the French national motto: "Liberty, equality, fraternity."

[85] *Verba et voces* "Words and voices"; cf. Horace, *Epistles* 1.1.34.

We are in favor of the defense of the human person, provided that it does not mean anything. We are in favor of defense of the human person, but we want to do to the Negroes what we reproach the Nazis for having done to the Jews. And not only to the Negroes, but to the Indochinese, the Madagascans, the Baltic peoples, the Germans of the Volga, etc. And not only to all these people, but to the proletariat of all the nations on which we claim to impose this official notion of respect for human dignity. The proletariat responds that in this notion it does not see anything which corresponds to respect for the proletariat. Thus, we defend and respect the human person, but an ideal human person, a human person *in abstracto*, a human person **in the sense understood by the Court.**

I know well that one requests that I not stop us here in a concern for these details. Putting things in order will come later. The universal conscience is for the moment occupied with the installation of its offices. But it is precisely the graphs pinned to the wall, the graphs of future development which worry me still more than the results thus far obtained. This quite naked human person, who does not have a fatherland and who is indifferent to any fatherland, who does not know the laws of the city and the odor of the city, but who perceives with a very personal instinct the international voice of the universal conscience, this new man, this dehydrated man, it is he whom I do not recognize. Your universal conscience protects a hothouse plant: this theoretical product, this industrial product has no more relationship to a man than a California orange wrapped in cellophane and transported across continents has to an orange on a tree. Both are an orange: but one has the taste of the ground, and it grows and exists on its tree according to the nature of things, and the other is nothing more than a product for human consumption. You have made of the human person a product for human consumption. It figures in statistics (faked besides), it is counted, it is exported, it is transported, it is insured, and when it is destroyed, it is paid for. I am at a total loss: that is not for me a **human person.**

When we think of a **human person**, we see a father with his children around him, with his children around his table, in a room on his farm, and he shares soup and bread with them, or in a house in the suburbs, and there is nowhere he's so well off as on his farm, or in his fourth floor apartment, or in his house in the suburbs, and he returns from work and he asks what happened that day; or he is in his workshop, and he shows to his little boy how one properly makes a board, how one passes one's hand over the board to check that the work is good. It is this human person whom we defend and respect, this human person and no other, and all that belongs to him, his children, his house, his work, his field. And we say that this human person has the right that his children's bread be assured, that his house be inviolable, that his work be honored, that his field belong to him. That his children's bread be assured, that means that a Negro, an Asian or a Semite will not dispute with him about the place to which he has a right inside the city, and that he will not be obliged some day, in order to live, to be the proletarian and the slave of a foreigner. That his house be inviolable, that means that he will be able to think what he wants and say what he wants, that he will be the Master at his table and the Master in his house, that he will be protected if he obeys the edicts of the prince, and that the Negro, the Asian or the Semite will not appear in front of his door to explain to him what it is necessary to think and to invite him to follow them to prison. That his work be honored, that means that he will meet with the men of his trade, those whom he calls his partners or his colleagues, as he wants, and that he will have the right to say that his work is hard, that the chair which he is making is worth so many pounds of bread, that each hour of his work is worth so many pounds of bread, that he has the right also to **live**, that is, not to wear worn-out shoes and torn clothing, to have his own radio if he so desires, to have his own house if he puts money aside for that, his own car if he succeeds in his work, the share of **luxury** that our machines owe him, and that the Negro, the Asian or the Semite will not fix at Winnipeg or Pretoria the price of his day's work and the menu at his table. And that his field belong to him, that means that he has the right to call himself the master of this house which his grandfather built, master of this city which his grandfather and those of the other men of the city built, that no one has the right to drive him out of his residence or out of the council house and that the foreign workmen whose grandfathers were not there when they built the belfry, the Negroes, the Asians and the Semites who work in the mine or who sell at the crossroads will not have at all the power to decide the destiny of his little boy. That is what we call the rights of the human person, and we say that the duty of the sovereign is nothing other than to ensure respect for these essential rights, and to manage his nation well, like a good father of a family as the rental leases say, like a father leads his family; that the laws are nothing other than wise rules, rules known by all, written with the help of the counsel of qualified men, posted on walls and sovereign; and that these rights, without which there is no city, must be defended by force if necessary, and in all cases by an effective protection. As one can see, we are in favor, we also, of the defense of the human person. But in these terms. And not **in the sense understood by the Court**. It is simply a matter of understanding oneself (*de se comprendre*).

This man of the earth and the cities, this man who has been **man** as long as there have been peoples and cities, it is precisely he that Nuremberg condemns and repudiates. For the new law says to him: "You will be a **citizen of the world**, you yourself will also be packaged and dehydrated, you will not listen anymore to the rustle of your trees and the voice of your bells, but you will learn to hear the voice of the universal conscience; shake the dirt (*terre*) from your shoes, peasant; this land (*terre*) is nothing any more; she soils, she obstructs, she prevents one from making pretty packagings. Modern times have come. Listen to the voice of modern times. The Polish laborer who changes jobs twelve times a year is the same man as you; the Jewish rag-hawker who has just arrived from Korotcha or Jitomir is the same man as you; they have the same rights as you on your land (*terre*) and on your city; respect the Negro, O peasant. They have the same rights as you, and you will set places for them at your table and they will enter into the council where they will teach you what the universal conscience says, which you do not yet hear as well as you should. And their sons will be respected men (*des messieurs*), and they will be established as judges over your sons; they will govern your city and they will buy your field, for the universal conscience gives them expressly all these rights. As for you, peasant, if you meet with your friends and long for the time when one saw only local boys at the city fair, know that you are opposing the universal conscience and that the law does not protect you against that."

For such, in truth, is the condition of man after the demotion of fatherlands. One perforce supports regimes that make cities wide open to strangers. One demands that these foreigners receive the same rights as the inhabitants of the country, and one condemns solemnly every attempt at discrimination. Then, one recognizes as legitimate only one manner of deliberation: that which is purely numerical. Under this system, what city will not be, in a given time, overcome by a peaceful conquest, swamped by an occupying army without uniforms and offered finally to the reign of foreigners?

The end result is thus attained. National differences will be little by little annihilated. International law will establish itself so much better than native law that the latter will no more have defenders. The national administrations which we were just describing take on in this perspective their true meaning: the States will be no more than administrative districts of a single Empire. And, from one end of the world to the other, in perfectly similar cities (since they will have been rebuilt after bombardments), there will live under similar laws a bastard population, a race of indefinable and gloomy slaves, without genius, without instinct, without voice. Dehydrated man will reign in a hygienic world. Immense bazaars echoing the sounds of record-players will symbolize this race of men of equal worth (*à prix unique*). Rolling sidewalks will run alongside the streets. They will transport every morning to their slave work the long line of the men without faces, and they will bring them back in the evening. And this will be the promised land. They will not know anymore, these users of the rolling sidewalks, that there was formerly a human condition. They will not know what were our cities, when they were our cities: no more than we can imagine what was Ghent or Bruges at the time of the aldermen. They will be astonished that the earth was beautiful and that we loved it passionately. For them, the universal conscience, clean, theoretical and die-cut in disks, will illuminate their skies. But this will be the promised land.

And above will reign in fact the **Human Person**, the one for whom this war was waged, the one who invented this law. For at last, no matter what one says, there is a **Human Person**. And this is not the Germans of the Volga, nor the people in the Baltics, nor is it the Chinese or the Malagasy, it's not the Annamese or the Czechs, and of course it's not the proletariat. The **Human Person**, we know very well what this is. This term has all its signification only (one can even say that it only has signification, **in the sense understood by the Court**) if it refers to a stateless individual, who was born in a Krakow suburb, who suffered under Hitler, was interned, is not dead, and has nonetheless been revived... in the form of a French, Belgian or Luxembourg patriot, on whom we are invited to bestow all our respect and adoration. The **Human Person**, in addition, is usually provided with an international passport, an authorization to export, a tax exemption and the right to requisition apartments. We might add that the **Human Person**, so defined, is most especially the agent (*dépositaire*) of the universal conscience: he is, so to speak, its electoral vase. For this role he possesses organs of an exquisite sensitivity which other men lack: thus in a country where he has just arrived, he designates with certainty the true **patriots** and detects at a great distance the organisms which stubbornly resist the vibrations of the universal conscience. Accordingly these precious gifts are used as is appropriate before public opinion.[86] All their vibratile reactions are carefully recorded and the total of these vibrations constitutes what one calls at a given moment the indignation or the approval of the universal conscience. They are what formulate finally the dogma which we already mentioned and which has as its title: **defense of the human person.**

It follows that the defense of the human person, in the sense understood by the Court, is a sort of mathematical truth, almost analogous to the Rule of Three.[87] One can express it thus: "Whoever is stateless and born at Krakow resides within the universal community, and every act which scratches or bruises them resounds deeply within the breast of the human conscience; to the extent that your specific definition distances you from being stateless in character and Krakowian in origin, you separate yourself from the universal community, and to that extent what bruises you has no longer a corresponding resonance in the human conscience. If you are resolutely hostile to the stateless individuals originally from Krakow, you are not at all part of the universal community, and one can do to you whatever one wants without the human conscience feeling the least bit hurt."

---

[86] "Aussi ces précieux dons sont-ils utilisés comme il convient devant l'opinion." Bardèche frequently uses *opinion* to mean "public opinion." His point here seems to be that these special gifts are used before the public for the sake of helping it to form public opinion.

[87] *Rule of Three* In mathematics, the "rule of three" is the method of finding the fourth term of a mathematical proportion when three terms are known.

These catechumens of the new humanity have customs that are sacred. They do not work the land, they do not produce anything, they find slavery repugnant. They do not mix with the men of the rolling sidewalk, they count them and direct them toward the tasks that are assigned to them. They do not at all wage war, but they like to establish themselves in brilliantly lit shops where in the evening they sell at a high price to the man of the rolling sidewalk what he has made and what they have bought from him at a low price. No one has the right to call them slave merchants and nevertheless the peoples in whose midst they are established work only for them. They form an order. It is this that they have in common with our former knighthoods. And is it not just that they are distinguished from other men, since they are the ones most sensitive to the voice of the universal conscience and furnish us the model which we must imitate? They have also their high priests in distant capitals. They revere in them the representatives of these illustrious families who have made themselves known by gaining a lot of money and by distributing a lot of advertising. And they themselves rejoice to read on the coats of arms of these heroes the amounts of their dividends. But these powerful men have great concerns. They meditate on the map of the world and decide that one such country will produce henceforth oranges, and another canons. Leaning on graphs, they channel around the millions of slaves of the rolling sidewalk, and they determine in their wisdom the number of shirts that they will be allowed to buy in a year and the number of calories that will be allocated to them in order to live. And the work of the other men circulates and is registered on the walls of their office as in those panels with transparent tubes in which run without stop various colored liquids. They are the stagehands of the universe. Who revolts against them speaks against the gods. They distribute and decide. And their servants, placed at intersections, receive their orders with gratitude, and they indicate to the man of the rolling sidewalk the direction in which to go. Thus works the world without borders, the world where everyone is at home, and which they have called the promised land.

* * * * *

Here is what is written in the verdict of Nuremberg.

And today even those who wrote this verdict turn toward German youth: "Germans, good Germans," they say to them, "don't you like the cause of Freedom? Aren't you ready to defend the world with us against Bolshevik barbarity? Germans, young Germans, would you not look good on long Sherman tanks, like dark gods of combat?" And their eyes fixed with rapture on a Germany at the same time Weimarian and invincible, peaceful and yet armed to the teeth, they cherish the dream of shock troops for democracy, Liberty's assault-troops, sentimental and intrepid, fair and muscular, docile as young girls but eternally engaged (*fiancés*) to the Declaration of Rights and ready to die for the Congress, the Occident, and the Y.M.C.A., a gigantic army of eunuchs who in combat would miraculously regain the strength of the Germans (*des Germains*).

It is necessary to know what one wants. We will not fight for clouds. Nor will the Germans apparently. The antidote for Bolshevism has borne a name in history. Let us cease to pronounce this name with fear and to look at this flag with horror. All ideas have something right about them.

Let us ask on what was based the power of this one. Instead of proscribing, let us try to understand. If millions of men were willing to get killed under this flag which we trample on so basely, is it not the case that it brought them some of the secret of life and of greatness which it is absurd for us not to want to know?

Our refusal to look at the writing on the wall is not only absurd, it is also infinitely dangerous. Ideological ruins are not like the ruins of cities: they are not seen, and travellers do not shake their heads seriously while passing by their debris. They are however more serious, they are mortal. The doctrines which we have madly struck with curses are the only ones which can provide a dam against the Communist flood. We have blown up the dam, and we are astonished now that the flood sweeps away the little walls with which we try to block it. It suffices however to look at the map. It is not reasonable to hope that the enormous sheet of land which extends from Asia to the Elbe will respect for long the fragile pontoon of the Occident. We are sure to be submerged if a powerful architecture does not make of the European peninsula an impregnable citadel, a kind of Gibraltar for the white race of the Occident.

But it is necessary to approach such tasks in the right frame of mind and to be reasonable. It is necessary to act here without passion and also without hypocrisy. We must forget this war and the sufferings that it brought us. We must forget our claims to be called the victors. The future will not be built on hatred or fear, nor on the humiliation of others. We must address ourselves to the new Germany and be trustworthy and honest in doing so. Our first task is to give up this falsification of history which we intend to impose. It is not true that Germany is responsible for this war: the responsibility of the warmongers in England and France is at least as heavy as the responsibility of Hitler. It is not true that the National-Socialist Party was a criminal conspiracy: it was a party of militants similar to other parties of militants in power, it was obliged to resort to force to defend its work and its effectiveness, as in dramatic circumstances all parties do which believe themselves to be in charge of the future of a great mission. It is not true that the Germans were "monsters": the nations which did not hesitate to buy their victory with the lives of 2,650,000 German civilians, that is, with 2,650,000 lives of German workmen, old men, women and children, do not have the right to direct this reproach at them. A dishonest investigation and a gigantic propaganda campaign have been able to deceive our consciences for a while. But the day will come when these same enemies of Germany may find it in their interest to restore the facts; blind Fortune will take Truth by the hand and will sit her down at the banquet table. We will acknowledge that we ought not to have allowed ourselves to deduce from occasional and generally individual misdeeds a condemnation of the entire regime, that the enemies of Germany also in conducting the war committed acts for which they should be prosecuted just like those whom we have condemned, and that we added to a shameful and most vile falsification of history the most dangerous of ideological masquarades.

We start to see today the extent of our fault. Everyone panics in front of this vacuum, this open hole in the center of Europe, and we look with terror at what we ourselves have done: Europe staggering like the blind Cyclops. This monstrous geographical mutilation, that is what everyone can see: another vacuum is not less grievous, another abyss exists, that which we created by brutally extirpating from the surface of the earth the only revolutionary system that one could oppose to Marxism. The universe of ideas is a universe which has its laws and its geography. It is as dangerous to brutally raze a whole ideological area as to destroy a nation. We abruptly reversed an ideological balance that time had arranged and which was not less necessary to the political health of Europe than was the existence of Germany to its strategic defense.

Let us not forget that what we have destroyed and condemned was, not only for the Germans but also for millions of men throughout the Occident, the only durable solution to the dilemma of the modern world, the only manner of escaping capitalist slavery without accepting Soviet slavery. What we destroyed was, in the minds of these men, not that reactionary and military tyranny which we pretend to denounce, but an immense effort at the emancipation of workers. Their red flag stamped with the sign of their fatherland was the emblem of the revolution of the Occident. We say that they were slaves even though they had the look of those who work joyfully. The looks on the workers' faces is a testimony: if they rebuild Stalingrad while singing, our anti- Communist newspapers lie about it; from the Baltic to the Brenner, you know well that the German workers were happy. And not only for German workers but for all the Occident, this new revolution was a signal and an immense cause for hope. It had not been carried out everywhere, it had not succeeded everywhere, but in all the countries it represented a chance for the future, which was **the** chance for the Occident, the annunciation to workers of a merry and strong life. We have said that they were mistaken, that they were misled. But what do we know about it? What is certain is that today in the desert that is the Occident they find nowhere else the revolutionary substance which the new nationalisms brought to them. This combat was for them greatness, fraternity, spilled blood, justice: yes, justice, in their hearts it was that, no matter what our courts say. It is forbidden for us to forget it, for us who speak to them. These words against which we have fiercely set ourselves, these gigantic blocks of will and hope which we have blown up like a piece of a continent, they were for millions of men as recently as yesterday the irrepressible call to nobility and sacrifice, they represented justice, long sought and finally found, a justice which is worth dying for. We have created a desert for hearts. Our policy in Europe has succeeded in making revolutionary enthusiasm something exclusively Soviet. After ten years of our potions, all the world's youth will be arranged under the red flag: to protest against injustice, we have left them only that. Let us return then to justice and probity. How much experience will we need to learn that just contracts are the only durable contracts, that right and honest peaces are the only peaces? In 1918, our statesmen learnedly upset the geography, and they were astonished to see a war come out of it. Today the same prigs take great trouble to destroy the European ideological balance: will they understand that this attack is no less grave and that a war will just as surely come out of it? It is essential that there exist in Europe a dynamic zone replete with social justice which crystallizes people's wills to resist Marxist annexation. Some men today have understood the enormous mistake they made in destroying the German army and industry: they think that the peninsula Europe needs a rampart. But it also needs a soul. The cry of anger which the men of our time raise against social injustice, against corruption and lies, it is necessary that the Occident echo it. This revolutionary will, this joy of the revolution marching along, must again be ours. Social justice is no less necessary to the Occident than steel and coal. If we do not have anything else to offer to workmen in our countrysides and in our cities than the usual democratic masquarades, no argument in the world will prevent them from looking with hope towards the land which speaks to them about emancipation and the power of the proletariat. We do not have the right to forget, and it would be insane to forget that this dream of a socialism proudly affirmed by the nation was that of millions of men in Europe. Truths are like fatherlands: they are not crushed by a boot kick. Whether we want it or not, this thought which was the great hope of yesterday, this fraternity of close combat, is today the natural basis for a community of the Occident.

For the safety of the new Europe and for our safety, our wills must therefore unite against this ideological diktat of Nuremberg which is no less deadly for the peace of the world than the political diktat of Versailles. We must return to fatherlands their crown and their sword. We must restore and proclaim the simple and natural principles of political wisdom. We must recall to the ferrymen of the clouds[88] that the sovereignty of cities, and all that that entails: the right to join with others and the right to banish, the primacy of discipline in the State, the absolute duty of obedience to those who are in the service of the sovereign, are the beams

---

[88] *the ferrymen of the clouds* a reference to the mythical ferryman of souls, Charon. The ideas (clouds) bandied about by modern politicians are as substanceless as the souls transported by Charon.

which support and which have always supported all nations. We must require the solemn recognition of this first truth which is the basis for all power: that he who obeys the prince and the edicts of the prince cannot be prosecuted, for there is no State without that, there is no government without that. We should not be afraid of strong States. And we do not have the right to require that the structure of these States be democratic (in the sense that the word is used in London or Washington) if these States prefer to live under other laws. If the unity of the Occident can be accomplished only around a block of authoritarian socialist States, is not this solution better than war and occupation?

For that is certainly what is at stake. In today's Europe, such States are the single guarantee of peace. Of course, at this moment, peace and the war do not depend on the European States: but they can become **the occasion** of war, and what one can ask of them is not to provide this occasion. However, it is only by a Western block where Communist agitation would be as impossible as is democratic agitation in the U.S.S.R. and where Communism would be impossible because National-Socialism would there be actualized, it is only by such a block that war can be averted. We need an iron curtain **around the Occident**. Because the danger of war lies not in the existence of States which are powerful and differently polarized like the United States and Soviet Russia; it lies on the contrary in the existence of weak zones open to competition between these two great powers, or, in other words, the danger of war increases with the possibilities of interference; war will be caused by agents from abroad who work among us. If, on the contrary, an Occidental block could be established, living by its own means as rigidly closed to American influence as to Communist influence, this neutral block, this impermeable citadel would be a factor for peace and perhaps for interaction. If the Europe of the Occident could become an island with steep cliffs which would live under its own laws and where neither the democratic spirit could be imported from the Americans, nor Communism imported from the Soviets, if this island were considered inaccessible and mortal, if it became strong, who would be interested in attacking it? After all, Western Europe has no fundamental strategic importance (other zones have much more), it has rather political importance for the belligerents, it is for the moment a *no man's land* which will belong to the most clever or quick. If we eliminate this competition, if we manage to free us from these conscientious ideologues, often self- interested, who attract bombs like a magnet attracts iron, is not this, for us and everyone, the best precondition for peace?

If America wants to make war tomorrow, these reflexions mean nothing: but in that case America will have created for itself strange conditions for war. But if we are permitted to count on the passage of some time, in what are these forecasts more absurd than others? This insularity of the Occident rests ultimately on a fundamental precondition. It will be necessary that the Americans be intelligent enough to understand that it is in their interest to arm Western Europe without asking from it in exchange any democratic allegiance. It is no small thing to say to them: give us planes and tanks, and then do not get disturbed if we throw out the door the agents from America as well as those from Moscow. Will they understand that it is in their interest as well as the Russians' that Western Europe be so constituted that it is at the same time anti- democratic and anti-communist, and that it be strong and jealous of its independence? Will they understand that this would be a great sign of wisdom and the beginning of real hope for peace: to exclude in the same manner those who, after having been the agents for England, now seek American subsidies, and those who receive their orders and their subsidies from Cominform?[89]

If the Americans want to erase the evil that they have done, let them erase it in their hearts, even as they seek to repair it today in the cities. If they want the Occident to be solid, let it be the Occident and not just an extension of America. It is only thus that it will become a political reality, for the American glacis[90] in Europe can only be a badly defended ground and, in the event of war, quickly evacuated. But the Empire of the Occident can exist and be defended, or at least it can establish its neutrality.

One starts to understand these things, but one understands them badly. Mrs. Roosevelt eloquently addresses German women to let them know that she admires their courage. These are fine condolences when one thinks of the bombardments ordered by her late husband. This tardy homage however informs us rather about the error of American policy: "I strike, then I arm; I condemn, then I raise." Blond Germans, don't you like the Lazard Bank? Bite the ground with your bloody mouths in pronouncing the

---

[89] *Cominform* the central bureau of the international Communist movement from 1947-1956.

[90] *Glacis* an open area that slopes down and away from a fixed fortification.

gentle names of Oppenheim and Kohn. But do you think that there will be numerous volunteers to form behind General de Gaulle a new anti-Bolshevik Legion or behind Marshal Montgomery the last SS brigade?

The Russians are less naive. They got rid of their most dangerous competitors. They impose on us via communist parties an intransigent condemnation of their opponents' cursed doctrines. At the same time, they convene the German generals to make them reconstitute a national army, and they put Mr. Wilhelm Pieck[91] on a platform to make him announce to the German people the birth of a new party "at once national and socialist." It is not I who put the words in this order: it is Communist propaganda which discovered this formula. It is up to us to know if we will fight

Communism with its own weapons or if we will always be too late, in regard to a war or an idea. I do not have an opinion about the third world war: besides it does not depend on us. But I believe there will be a quick and decisive battle (*une bataille sèche*) for control of the Occident. The winner of this battle will be, as formerly, he whom the Franks of Germany will hoist on their shields.

As for us, our imagination is always so brilliant. Our weekly magazines make inquiries to ask us what we will do if we are occupied by the Russians. We are quite optimistic. We have not yet seen that, as things are going, chances are

---

[91] *Wilhelm Pieck* a pre-war German Communist and Stalin crony who became the first president of the German Democratic Republic.

just as good that we will be occupied by soldiers whom we know already. Let us look directly at the future which awaits us. We can save everything by making the Occident; we are nothing any more if a Communist administration over the Occident is established against us. Our destiny is being played out this moment in Germany. It is necessary for us to choose to have the SS either with us or over us (*avec nous ou chez nous*).

Maurice Bardèche

OTHER TITLES

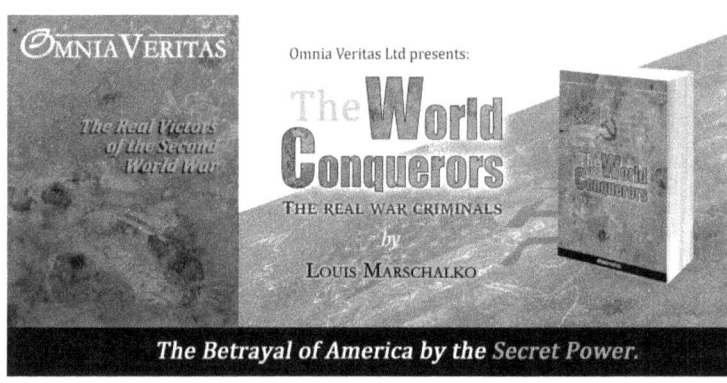
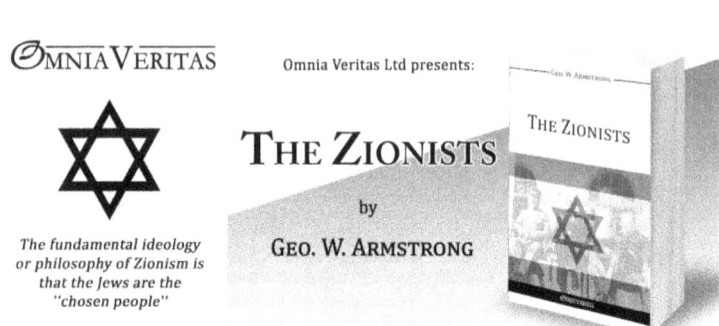

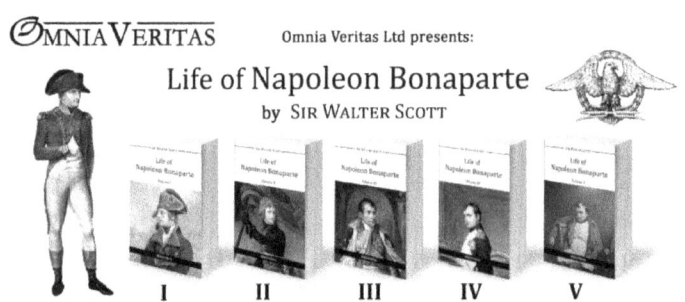

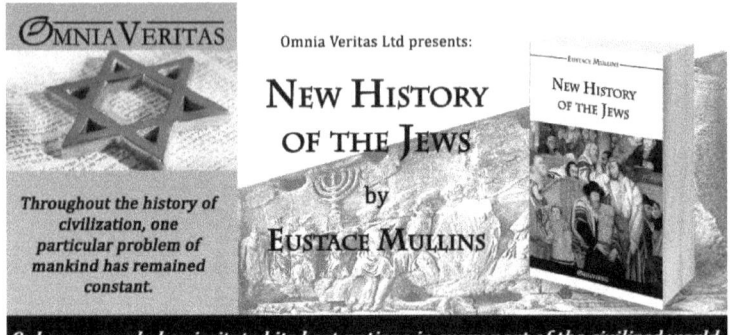

www.omnia-veritas.com

www.ingramcontent.com/pod-product-compliance
Lightning Source LLC
Chambersburg PA
CBHW060819190426
43197CB00038B/2078